DATE DUE

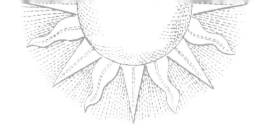

THE GREAT
HISPANIC HERITAGE

Gabriel García Márquez

THE GREAT HISPANIC HERITAGE

Isabel Allende

Miguel de Cervantes

César Chávez

Salvador Dalí

Gabriel García Márquez

Dolores Huerta

Frida Kahlo

José Martí

Pedro Martinez

Ellen Ochoa

Pablo Picasso

Juan Ponce de León

Diego Rivera

Carlos Santana

Sammy Sosa

Pancho Villa

THE GREAT
HISPANIC HERITAGE

Gabriel García Márquez

Susan Muaddi Darraj

CHELSEA HOUSE
PUBLISHERS
An imprint of Infobase Publishing

Gabriel García Márquez

Copyright © 2006 by Infobase Publishing

All rights reserved. No part of this book may be reproduced or utilized in any form or by any means, electronic or mechanical, including photocopying, recording, or by any information storage or retrieval systems, without permission in writing from the publisher. For information contact:

Chelsea House
An imprint of Infobase Publishing
132 West 31st Street
New York NY 10001

Library of Congress Cataloging-in-Publication Data

Darraj, Susan Muaddi.
  Gabriel García Márquez / Susan Muaddi Darraj.
    p. cm. — (The great Hispanic heritage)
  Includes bibliographical references and index.
  ISBN 0-7910-8839-1 (hardcover)
  1. García Márquez, Gabriel, 1928- 2. Authors, Colombian—20th century—
Biography. I. Title. II. Series.
  PQ8180.17.A73Z6543 2006
  863'.64—dc22   2006010615

Chelsea House books are available at special discounts when purchased in bulk quantities for businesses, associations, institutions, or sales promotions. Please call our Special Sales Department in New York at (212) 967-8800 or (800) 322-8755.

You can find Chelsea House on the World Wide Web at http://www.chelseahouse.com

Text design by Terry Mallon, Keith Trego
Cover design by Keith Trego

Printed in the United States of America

Bang EJB 10 9 8 7 6 5 4 3 2 1

This book is printed on acid-free paper.

All links and Web addresses were checked and verified to be correct at the time of publication. Because of the dynamic nature of the Web, some addresses and links may have changed since publication and may no longer be valid.

Table of Contents

1   Taking a Risk   6

2   Life in Aracataca   9

3   A Tense Courtship   16

4   Living with the Colonel   25

5   Finding His Calling   34

6   Life in Bogotá   40

7   A Fallen Hero   48

8   Stranded in Europe   62

9   The Cuban Revolution   68

10 Writing the Masterpiece   76

11 Politics and the Nobel Prize   83

    Chronology and Timeline   98

    Notes   102

    Bibliography   105

    Further Reading   108

    Index   109

Taking
a Risk

Surely, people said, Gabo had gone mad.

It was 1965 in Mexico City, and most of his friends and neighbors had not seen novelist and journalist Gabriel García Márquez in months. This was highly unusual, since "Gabo"—as he was affectionately called—had a reputation as a friendly and sociable person.

Rumors circulated that he had secluded himself and was working feverishly on a new novel. These rumors were confirmed by García Márquez's wife, Mercedes, who protected her husband as he wrote and, in accordance with his wishes, prevented all interruptions and distractions. However, the months passed and he still had not finished the book about which people were speculating. While she gave excuses and patiently explained that Gabo needed space and privacy to write, Mercedes also worried privately about the lack of money coming in. She had two children—Rodrigo and Gonzalo—for whom to care and provide. To offset the lack of income and mounting bills, she resorted to selling the

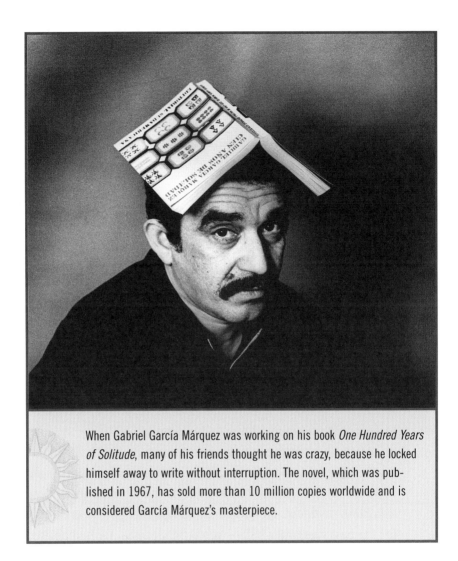

When Gabriel García Márquez was working on his book *One Hundred Years of Solitude*, many of his friends thought he was crazy, because he locked himself away to write without interruption. The novel, which was published in 1967, has sold more than 10 million copies worldwide and is considered García Márquez's masterpiece.

family's furniture and car. She refrained, however, from expressing her financial concerns to her husband as he wrote draft after draft of his novel.

Working full time on a new book posed not only a financial dilemma for García Márquez, but a creative and psychological one as well. He had reached a point in his career where his motivation to write fiction had come to a sudden, jarring halt. The problem had begun after the 1962 publication of his novella *In Evil Hour*, which had suffered from a poor editing job. After recovering from his initial disappointment, García

Márquez had found himself unable to write creatively with his usual enthusiasm.

This kind of dry period spelled danger for García Márquez, who had dropped out of law school against his family's wishes to become a writer. Writing for newspapers helped him establish a name for himself in journalism, but writing articles and short stories did not pay very well—nowhere near enough to support a young family.

Nonetheless, he knew that his real talent lay in creative writing, not journalism. Despite knowing how poorly the field paid, García Márquez pursued his ambition. He wanted to write novels like the ones that had inspired him, such as the works of William Faulkner, Jorge Luis Borges, and Ernest Hemingway.

The idea for the novel he was working on now had been brewing in his mind for years. He wanted to write an epic novel, one that would tell the modern history of Colombia in a focused way, through the inhabitants of a small village named Macondo. When the idea finally struck him, he decided to devote every waking hour to its completion.

After 18 months, secluded in his home and with his family on the verge of financial ruin, García Márquez finally emerged with his completed novel in hand. Now he worried about how this book—which had sucked up all his energy and creativity for the past year and a half—would be received. He had poured all his talent into it. Its success could mark a steep ascent in his career, but its failure would trigger a downward spiral from which he might never recover.

2

Life in Aracataca

The life of Gabriel García Márquez is a story of amazing successes and shattering disappointments, but it is impossible to understand his life and work without recognizing the importance of his social, political, and ethnic background, rooted in his native country of Colombia.

Colombia is a small nation, but one that has a wide variety of climates. The differences result from the various elevations of the land: Depending on whether a Colombian city is located by the coast, in the middle of the country, or in the mountains, its temperature may be hot, mild, or cold. Most of the country lies in a hot zone, because Colombia has a long coastline, but its capital city, Bogotá, is in the colder highlands area. The Andes Mountains also prominently mark the landscape of the nation.

THE HISTORY OF ARACATACA

Aracataca, where García Márquez was born, is a small town, founded in the late 1800s on the Caribbean coast by people who were

The nation of Colombia, where Gabriel García Márquez was born, has a unique landscape that features both a long coast and the rugged terrain of the Andes Mountains, pictured here.

fleeing the chaos of Colombia's civil war, known as the War of a Thousand Days. The name is taken from the river Ara, in the language of the Chimila Indians who settled the region; the second part of the town's name, "Cataca," is the word for the title of the town's leader. In his memoir, *Living to Tell the Tale*, García Márquez notes, "Therefore we natives do not call it Aracataca but use its correct name: Cataca."[1] Aracataca sits in the coastal region of Colombia. As Raymond Williams, a biographer of García Márquez explains, the coastal region is a mix of African and Hispanic ethnic cultures and enclaves, making the local culture vibrant and exotic.[2]

The town was most prosperous between 1915 and 1918, when the United Fruit Company (now known as Chiquita

International) established itself in the region. A North American company, United Fruit specialized in growing and selling bananas, and set up banana plantations across the region. According to Mario Vargas Llosa, the Peruvian novelist,

THE MULTIFACETED CARIBBEAN COAST OF COLOMBIA

Colombia has two coastal regions. The southwestern part of the country lies along the Pacific Ocean, while the northern region is on the coast of the Caribbean Sea. The Caribbean coastal region, which includes cities like Barranquilla and Cartagena, as well as García Márquez's hometown of Aracataca, differs significantly in climate and culture from other parts of Colombia. The coastal region is warm and tropical. It is also a crossroads of many different cultures, including African, Indian, and Spanish ethnicities.

Cartagena, for example, was the first slave port in the Americas, and Africans were brought there to be bought and sold at slave auctions. Other immigrants have arrived over the years and diversified the region's culture even more. The Caribbean coast is also a region where imagination and creativity are encouraged in the form of local legends and superstitions, which García Márquez's grandmother frequently recounted for him.

"This region is viewed even by Colombians as a distinct and exotic part of the nation," writes Raymond Williams, a biographer of García Márquez. "It is still common for males in this region, for example, to support several women and father thirty or forty children."* It is not surprising, then, that in *One Hundred Years of Solitude*, García Márquez created a character named Colonel Aureliano Buendia, who has many, many sons, all named after him, by different mothers.

* Raymond Williams, *Gabriel García Márquez* (Boston: Twayne Publishers, 1984), 7.

Loading docks such as this one were used by the United Fruit Company to ship bananas to distant ports in the United States and Europe. The UFCO, which later became Chiquita, held a virtual monopoly over the banana trade in parts of Central and South America during the early part of the twentieth century.

journalist, and literary critic, "Many fortunes grew under the shade of banana trees"[3] and many people quickly became wealthy as a result of the booming economy. However, while many jobs were created, many workers were treated poorly and paid unfairly low wages. The blame for the social inequity was placed on the landowners who became wealthy overnight but treated their fellow countrymen poorly, and especially on the United Fruit Company itself. Colombians accused the company of creating an employment situation where workers could be treated terribly while investors raked in profits.

In 1928, some banana workers, tired and frustrated with the system, decided to go on strike against the United Fruit Company. However, the Colombian government, corrupt and eager not to upset a key foreign investor, worked closely with the company to repress the workers' strike. The result was the infamous Santa Marta Massacre, in which hundreds of peaceful protesters were gunned down and killed by the Colombian

THE SANTA MARTA MASSACRE

In the fall of 1928, more than 32,000 banana plantation workers went on strike against the United Fruit Company. The workers had been complaining about unfair treatment for several years, but the company's response had never satisfied them. In 1928, the leaders of the various workers' unions presented the company with a list of demands, which included higher wages and more sanitary working conditions. The company refused to meet these demands, so a strike was called.

In December 1928, a crowd gathered in the public square in the city of Ciénaga, Colombia, not far from Aracataca, to support the strikers and to call upon the United Fruit Company to meet the workers' demands. Word of the demonstration reached the government. Alarmed military authorities sent troops, led by General Carlos Cortés Vargas, to keep peace at the event.

The troops, however, fired upon the crowds of peaceful demonstrators, killing hundreds of them. Known as *La masacre de las bananeras* [the massacre of the banana workers], it was the worst and most violent repression of the labor movement in Colombia's history. The killing shocked the nation and sparked heavy criticism of the conservative government. When elections were held in 1930, the Conservative Party lost and the Liberal Party took control of the government.

The massacre was censored out of history books in Colombia for many years, but Gabriel García Márquez mentioned it in his novel *One Hundred Years of Solitude*. García Márquez describes *La masacre de las bananeras* in a scene that has been hailed as one of the finest examples of literature recreating history.

Army. This episode would be told and retold through generations. It was especially poignant to the grandfather of Gabriel García Márquez, who frequently recounted the story to his young grandson.

THE MÁRQUEZ LEGACY

García Márquez's maternal grandparents moved to Aracataca around 1911, when his mother was five years old, and built a home for their family in the small town. The house, as García Márquez described it later in his memoir, was "linear," with "eight successive rooms along a hallway with an alcove filled with begonias where the women in the family would sit to embroider on frames and talk in the cool of the evening."[4] The reason for the Márquez family's move to Aracataca is shrouded in mystery: In the town where they had previously lived, García Márquez's grandfather, Nicolás Ricardo Márquez Meja, a former colonel in the army, had allegedly killed a man during a duel. Filled with remorse over what he had done, he had packed his family's belongings and moved out of town to Aracataca.

The family arrived in Aracataca shortly before the banana boom and were some of the town's earliest residents. The boom lasted until after World War I ended, in 1918. After the war, many of the banana companies left the region or reduced their investment, and the economy of Aracataca and other small coastal villages began to decline. The decline was not only financial, but also social and political. "The town was assaulted by outlaws, decimated by epidemics, [and] ravaged by deluges,"[5] writes Mario Vargas Llosa. These disasters, aggravated by the poverty that afflicted the area, lasted only a few years, and then Aracataca settled into a quiet rhythm, with a reduced population and a ruined economy. In the eyes of many people, especially Colonel Nicolás Márquez Meja, the United Fruit Company had rumbled through, exploited the land, and then left the local population to pick up the pieces.

The stamp left upon Aracataca and the Caribbean coastal region by the United Fruit Company occurred years before the birth of Gabriel García Márquez, but it would become a major influence on his personal vision of his country—and thus on his literary work.

A Tense Courtship

The Márquez family was not wealthy, but they enjoyed a widely held respect and high social status among the citizens of Aracataca, because they helped found the town. No real problems rattled the family, until their daughter decided that she was in love.

García Márquez's mother, Luisa Santiaga Márquez Iguarán, was much loved by her parents, having been born shortly after the death of her grandmother, for whom she was named. Her parents spent much time and energy on young Luisa, giving her piano lessons and trying to turn her into a respectable young lady.

AN UNSAVORY SUITOR

Luisa was an energetic and romantic young girl and she soon fell in love with Gabriel Eligio García—a young telegraph operator whom her parents did not like. The list of reasons the family disliked Luisa's suitor was quite lengthy. Not only was he poor, but he was one of the people who had moved to Aracataca after the

16

banana boom, unlike the Márquez family, who helped found the town. This latter reason led the Márquez family to refer to the young suitor as *la hojarasca*, which means a "dead leaf," "as in something that descends in useless flurries and is best swept away."[6] A former medical student who had to drop out of school because he did not have enough money, young Gabriel Eligio García became a telegraph operator so he could earn a living. He traveled to different towns looking for work, but never settled in one place for very long. He did not have a lineage prestigious enough to satisfy Luisa Márquez's parents, who had high hopes and ambitions for the young woman.

The list of reasons not to like him did not end there. García not only came from humble stock, but he had been born out of wedlock. The story was that his mother had given birth to him when she was only 14 years old, after a tryst with a local schoolteacher. She later went on to have seven other children, by different fathers, without ever marrying any of them.[7] The Márquez family saw this as further proof of García's unworthiness. Furthermore, since his arrival in Aracataca, García had quickly gained a reputation as a womanizer. García Márquez later wrote of his father:

> A photograph from those days shows him … wearing a suit of dark taffeta with a four-button jacket, very close-fitting in the style of the day, a high stiff collar and wide tie, and a flat-brimmed straw hat. He also wore fashionable round spectacles with thin wire frames and clear lenses. Those who knew him at the time saw him as a hard-living, womanizing bohemian who nonetheless never drank alcohol or smoked a cigarette in his long life.[8]

In truth, the local telegraph operator had earned his unsavory reputation. He had fathered four illegitimate children before he even met Luisa Márquez. Her parents certainly knew this, and it was one of the main reasons why they objected to their daughter's involvement with him. Most of the towns-people agreed: As García Márquez himself says, "The majority of adults . . . viewed Luisa Santiaga as the precious jewel of a rich and powerful family whom a parvenu telegraph operator was courting not for love but self-interest."[9]

Perhaps the most serious offense of all, in the eyes of Colonel Nicolás Márquez, was that his daughter's suitor was a member of the Conservative Party. The colonel himself was a staunch Liberal, having fought on the side of the Liberal's cause in the War of a Thousand Days, Colombia's bloody civil war, which was fought between the Conservatives and Liberals and raged between 1899 and 1902. The Conservatives and Liberals were Colombia's two main political parties, and the tension and hostility between the rivals was decades old.

Luisa Márquez, however, had her own reasons for falling in love with the young man who so displeased her parents: She had an artistic soul, and so did he. He played the violin, sang, read poetry, and courted her persistently. At a dance they both attended one evening, he surprised her with a rose, saying simply, "I give you my life in this rose."[10] After that, Luisa Márquez could not stop thinking about him, and she fought with her parents, demanding to be allowed to marry him.

The courtship was long, awkward, and filled with tension. The Márquez family spurned García in every way. Once, when he visited their home along with several other young people, everyone was asked to be seated—except Gabriel García, who was left to stand alone, awkward and embarrassed. Another time, he purchased a revolver to protect himself, knowing Colonel Márquez's reputation as a soldier and the notoriety of his violent temper.[11] Nevertheless, he never allowed himself to be intimidated by these tactics, and he pursued Luisa as ardently as ever. The young couple met in secret whenever possible and wrote letters that were carried between them by sympathetic friends and family members.

Luisa eventually convinced the vicar, or clergyman, of the local church diocese to speak to her parents on their behalf. He

There are no precise records of the year in which Gabriel García Márquez was born. Most people believe it was 1927, the year this photograph of Barranquilla, Colombia—a city that would be very important in García Márquez's life—was taken.

did, telling Colonel Nicolás Márquez and his wife that they should not interfere in the love of a couple who wanted so badly to be together. Aracataca's vicar was quite an influential person, highly respected by the community. Eventually, he won the grudging consent of Luisa's parents. The wedding of Luisa Márquez and Gabriel García took place on June 11, 1926, though the ceremony was not attended by the parents of the bride, who had consented but were still resentful.[12]

The newlyweds sailed to and settled in Riohacha, a nearby town, where Gabriel García had been offered a full-time job as the local telegraph operator. The couple soon returned to

Aracataca, after Luisa became pregnant a couple of months after the wedding. Her parents wanted their daughter close to them, and invited the couple to move into their home. Reluctantly, Gabriel García allowed his wife to move in with her family, where they could care for her during her pregnancy, while he continued working. His father-in-law was moved by this gracious act and offered his financial support, telling his son-in-law, "I am prepared to give you all the satisfactions that may be necessary."[13]

A WRITER IS BORN

Gabriel García Márquez was reportedly born on March 6, 1927. (Because no birth certificates were issued in the village at that time, some sources state that he was born in 1928; therefore, the date of his birth remains a mystery.) Later, his family told him that he had nearly died during birth, as the midwife "lost control of her art at the worst possible moment"[14] and almost allowed him to be strangled by the umbilical cord. García Márquez was born unconscious, but was revived when someone poured holy water on him. (Infant mortality rates were high in those days, and since Catholics believed that an unbaptized soul may not enter heaven, blessed water was usually kept on hand at births, in case a baby needed to be baptized quickly.)

Naming the baby proved to be a complicated task. He should have been named Olegario, García Márquez writes, "the saint whose day it was, but nobody had the saints' calendar near at hand, and with a sense of urgency they gave me my father's first name followed by that of Jose, the Carpenter, because he was the patron saint of Aracataca and March was his month."[15] A third name, Concordia, was added to signify "the general reconciliation achieved among families and friends with my arrival into the world,"[16] probably to mark the compromise that seemed to have been reached between Luisa's parents and their son-in-law. However, when he was officially baptized three years later,

Gabriel Jose de la Concordia was actually named Gabriel Jose García Márquez—the third part, "Concordia," had been dropped.

After the birth of their son, Luisa and Gabriel decided to allow her parents to care for the baby. After several entrepreneurial attempts ended in failure, Gabriel García needed to find a job, and Aracataca did not need a telegraph operator. Besides, he hoped to start a pharmacy, where he might be able to put some of his former medical training to use. Such an endeavor, however, required time and travel, which was difficult with a young infant.

It was not unusual for grandparents to raise their grandchildren in those days. Therefore, for the first eight years of his life, Gabo, as he was called (the nickname comes from Gabito, meaning "little Gabriel," to distinguish him from his father), grew up with his grandparents in Aracataca while his parents worked in other cities, trying to make money for the future of their young family.

CREATIVE INFLUENCES

Growing up in the home of his maternal grandparents (which is now a museum dedicated to García Márquez and his work)[17] was undoubtedly one of the major factors in García Márquez's later decision to become a writer. The Márquez home in the small village of Aracataca provided the young boy with ample material to inspire and develop his imagination.

Later, as an adult, García Márquez would specifically cite the influence of his grandmother Tranquilina's storytelling abilities. She was a talented orator with a wild imagination. She believed that spirits and ghosts lived in her house, and her grandson "sometimes . . . saw his grandmother chatting naturally with ghosts who came to visit her."[18] She also served as a storehouse of all the ancient tales, legends, and superstitions of the town of Aracataca. She would often invent fantastic reasons and explanations for everyday occurrences. For example, she would be suddenly stunned if she saw that, while doing her housekeeping, the rocking chairs rocked alone, that the phantom of puerperal fever was lurking in the bedrooms of women in labor, that the scent of jasmines from the garden was like an invisible ghost, that a cord dropped by accident on the floor had the shape of the numbers that might be the grand prize in the lottery, that a bird without eyes had wandered into the dining room and could be chased away by singing *La Magnifica*.[19]

She created fantastic reasons to explain these phenomena, such as spirits from the afterlife and creatures with magical powers.

GABRIEL GARCÍA MÁRQUEZ'S LEGACY

MAGICAL REALISM

Many writers and readers have been fascinated by García Márquez's writing style, in which he often conflates reality with fantasy. For example, in his novel *One Hundred Years of Solitude*, García Márquez describes the way in which a character named Remedios the Beauty, who bears a supernatural type of allure for the men in the town, is lifted into the air by a mysterious wind and carried away. In the scene, Ursula, the village chief's wife, watches transfixed as Remedios the Beauty rises through the sky:

> Ursula, almost blind at the time, was the only person who was sufficiently calm to identify the nature of the light as she watched Remedios the Beauty waving goodbye in the midst of the flapping sheets that rose up with her, abandoning with her the environment of beetles and dahlias and passing through the air with her as four o'clock in the afternoon came to an end, and they were lost forever with her in the upper atmosphere where not even the highest-flying birds of memory could reach her.*

This line is a perfect example of the literary genre—magical realism—that García Márquez helped shape. The genre embodies an

Tranquilina Márquez believed in the prophetic power of dreams and spent much of her time interpreting her own dreams and those of her friends and family. She enjoyed describing her dreams in detail to her impressionable grandson. In addition, she could tell tall tales with such directness and simplicity that García Márquez (and other people in the small community) could not help but believe her, despite the wild nature of the stories themselves.

Many of her imaginings—both daytime and nocturnal—made their way into García Márquez's later writing. They also deeply influenced his literary style. He once said:

alternative vision of reality, in which the author represents the many realities that exist. Dreams, superstitions, and personal anecdotes all have their own reality. There is no single, objective "truth."

García Márquez often discusses the origin of magical realism in his work. It had many different influences. One was the voice of his grandmother, who raised him in the village of Aracataca. She often told him fantastic stories and recounted local legends, but delivered the information in a serious tone. In other words, she presented fiction as fact, never distinguishing between the two. Another influence on his style was the work of Franz Kafka, the German author who wrote *The Metamorphosis*, a story that opens with the main character waking up to find himself transformed into a giant cockroach. Despite its unbelievable premise, the story proceeds in a matter-of-fact manner.

For García Márquez, what matters most in his work is not "the truth," but rather one's recollection of what is true. The personal memories of characters are as important—if not more so—than the actual events that occurred.

*   Gabriel García Márquez, *One Hundred Years of Solitude* (New York: Harper Perennial, 2004), 255.

If you say that there are elephants flying in the sky, people are not going to believe you. But if you say that there are four hundred and twenty-five elephants in the sky, people will probably believe you. . . . When I was very small there was an electrician who came to the house. I became very curious because he carried a belt with which he used to suspend himself from the electrical posts. My grandmother used to say that every time this man came around, he would leave the house full of butterflies. But when I was writing this, I discovered that if I didn't say that the butterflies were yellow, people would not believe it.[20]

Thus, García Márquez learned to write about magical events in specific ways, which would later become a hallmark of his style.

While Tranquilina Márquez spun incredible stories and infused those around her with a respect for dreams and ghosts, the real storyteller in the Márquez family home in Aracataca was García Márquez's grandfather. Colonel Nicolás Márquez was an imposing figure in the household. Besides his young grandson, he was the only other male in a home inhabited by Tranquilina, three aunts, and a bevy of female servants. "In the midst of that troop of evangelical women, my grandfather was complete security for me," García Márquez writes. "My doubts disappeared only with him, and I felt I had my feet on the ground and was well established in real life."[21] Although his grandmother's world of superstition, ghosts, and fantastic dreams intrigued him, García Márquez often sought the dominating presence of the person he would later call "the most important figure in my life."[22]

4

Living with the Colonel

Colonel Nicolás Ricardo Márquez Meja was a veteran of the War of a Thousand Days. His war stories fascinated his grandson and helped Gabo appreciate politics and history. The colonel explained the political aspects of the war to his grandson, detailing how the Liberals and Conservatives fought over control of the government and its handling of the economy.

LEGACY OF A WAR

The actual difference between the Liberals and Conservatives is negligible, although years of tension resulting from those differences made the two groups bitter enemies and rivals for power in Colombia. In 1821, Simón Bolívar, the man who liberated Colombia from Spanish colonial rule, created Colombia's first constitution, which established a strong central government. His ally and successor, Francisco de Paula Santander, ruled with a weaker central government. Essentially, those who supported Bolívar's political

A civil war, called the War of a Thousand Days, raged in Colombia between 1899 and 1902. This photograph of Colombian soldiers was taken toward the end of the fighting, in 1902.

philosophy were Conservatives, and those who advocated Santander's idea of a weaker government (called "federalism"), in which local states have more authority, were called Liberals. However, both parties wanted Colombia to succeed. Leslie Jermyn, author of a book on Colombia's history, writes, "Although their methods differed, the parties had somewhat similar goals, and people tended to support whichever party their parents supported."[23] Sometimes, however, tensions ran high and divided people.

The civil war and the bitter feud between the political parties had split the nation, even tearing families apart. In fact, at one point, the colonel himself had been captured and imprisoned by his wife's first cousin. Tranquilina Márquez was upset at the news and prayed for his safe return, but when she found out that her husband was also being humiliated by being held in stocks, she lost her temper. When she became angry, Tranquilina could become consumed by "a mood that," as her grandson explained it, "in no way corresponded to her name." The fiery-tempered Tranquilina marched to the prison, "confronted her cousin with a whip and forced him to turn my grandfather over to her safe and sound,"[24] writes García Márquez. Many such personal stories made the colonel's retelling of the war's overall history more colorful.

García Márquez's grandfather taught him Colombian history and inspired in him a respect for leaders like Simón Bolívar. He encouraged his grandson to be artistic and to draw, although young García Márquez provoked the anger and outrage of his grandmother and aunts by drawing on the walls of the home for a lack of paper. Colonel Márquez also taught his grandson the power of language. One day, he took Gabo to a circus. When García Márquez pointed out one animal in particular, the colonel told him that it was a camel. However, a bystander overheard the exchange and corrected the colonel, saying, "Excuse me, Colonel, but it's a dromedary." Embarrassed to have appeared ignorant in front of his grandson, the colonel went home that day and looked up the word *dromedary* in the dictionary. Then he gave the dictionary to García Márquez, saying, "This book not only knows everything, but it's also the only one that's never wrong."

García Márquez asked, "How many words does it have?"

His grandfather replied, "All of them."

This answer sparked a curiosity in the boy about words
(continued on page 30)

HOW COLOMBIA'S POLITICAL TURBULENCE AFFECTED GABRIEL GARCÍA MÁRQUEZ

Colombia's political history, so important to the life and work of Gabriel García Márquez, can only be described as being filled with turbulence and upheaval. Having declared independence from Spain in 1810, Colombia is one of the oldest democracies in Latin America, but, as writer Allen B. Ruch notes, "the sad fact is that this 'democracy' has rarely known peace and justice."* Colombia fell under the control of a dictator in 1815, but was then liberated again by Simón Bolívar in 1819. The country became advanced politically, and two distinct political parties formed: the Liberals and the Conservatives. Unfortunately, these two parties did not promote the ideal of democracy in Colombia. Instead, they were responsible for centuries of bloodshed.

In 1899, the two warring political factions engaged in what became known as the War of a Thousand Days, a civil war that led to the deaths of more than 100,000 people. The dispute began over the falling price of coffee. The Conservatives, who were in control of the government at the time, panicked because of the declining economy and issued paper money that was not backed by gold. As a result, the value of the peso decreased dramatically, forcing coffee farmers into bankruptcy and leading the Liberals to declare war on the government. The war raged for three years. The Liberals eventually lost, but the two parties negotiated a settlement in 1902 that promised economic and political reform.

The peace did not last long, as the decades-old hostilities between the Liberals and the Conservatives exploded again in 1948. That was the year that Jorge Eliécer Gaitán, a popular Liberal politician, was assassinated—as many alleged—as the result of a Conservative plot. Bogotá fell into a period of chaos and 2,500 people died in three days of rioting. Known as *La violencia*, the rioting eventually led to an all-out war that spread throughout the country. Within five years, more than

150,000 people were killed. In 1953, a military coup led by General Gustavo Rojas Pinilla, overthrew the Conservative government under President Laureano Gómez. In 1957, Pinilla was overthrown by another military coup, and the Liberals and Conservatives agreed to form a National Front, in which they would share power, alternating the presidency between the two parties.

Both the War of a Thousand Days—which occurred before García Márquez was born—and *La violencia*—which he experienced firsthand—deeply affected the author's work and perspective. His identity as a Colombian was shaped by these two events, and his feelings about politics and power, which are major themes in his novels, can be traced back to these turbulent events.

The situation has not improved in modern times. Political groups, whose aim is to transform Colombia from a capitalist nation to a socialist one, have been trying to overthrow the government since the 1960s. They have funded their efforts by participating in the drug trade. Colombia exports large amounts of illegal drugs, especially cocaine, and this has proven to be one of the most devastating developments in the history of modern Colombia. The insurgency, which has also committed high-profile kidnappings to gain funding, has put a great deal of pressure on the nation's government. Negotiations have fallen apart time after time, and the future of the nation is unclear.

As a supporter of socialism, Gabriel García Márquez has written frequently about Colombia's current political turmoil, and has even been invited to help in the negotiation processes. Colombian and international leaders often ask his advice on political matters.

* Allen B. Ruch, "The Uncertain Old Man Whose Real Existence Was the Simplest of His Enigmas." Available online at *www.themodern-world.com/gabo/gabo_biography.html*

Simón Bolívar was born in Venezuela in 1783. During his lifetime, he helped win the independence of his own country and several others in South America, including Colombia, which gained its independence in 1819.

(continued from page 27)

and their meanings, and he read the dictionary as if it were a novel, even though he did not understand much of what he read. Nevertheless, he later wrote, "That was my first contact with what would be the fundamental book in my destiny as a writer."[25]

García Márquez's grandfather was in excellent health, despite his old age. He worked ambitiously around the house, maintaining the property with great care and attention, and never missed Sunday Mass at the local Catholic church. However, he did suffer from physical ailments, many of them old war wounds that flared up occasionally into aches and pains. Also, when García Márquez was still a child, his grandfather lost sight in his right eye and had to wear an eye patch, which he later traded in for a pair of spectacles. He relied on a walking stick to help him get around, and he was never seen without it. Despite these setbacks, he remained a powerful presence in Gabo's life.

FAMILY REUNION

García Márquez's grandfather's influence could not last forever. When he was eight years old, García Márquez's fantasy life in Aracataca ended when his grandfather suddenly died. At the time, García Márquez was actually away from Aracataca, visiting his parents. García Márquez's father had decided to move his family, which now included other children in addition to Gabo (he would eventually have 10 younger siblings), to his own hometown of Sincé, where he hoped to open a pharmacy. As they reunited in Sincé, the family received a telegram that the colonel had become ill with a throat infection, which was soon discovered to be cancer. He died soon thereafter.

García Márquez was initially unaffected emotionally. He stayed in Sincé and enrolled in school there. Several months later, when the family returned to Aracataca after the pharmacy failed, García Márquez witnessed the family ritual of burning his grandfather's possessions. A huge bonfire was lit in the courtyard and his clothing was tossed into the flames. "His *liquiliques* [suits] and the white linen he wore as a civilian colonel resembled him as if he were still alive inside them while they burned,"[26] he wrote. That was when the tremendous personal loss of his grandfather struck the young boy, and he realized how much his grandfather had meant to him.

By the mid-1930s, the García Márquez family consisted of three boys—Gabo being the eldest—and three girls, in addition to mother Luisa and father Gabriel. Without the support and the stable presence of his grandfather, and with grandmother Tranquilina's health deteriorating rapidly, García Márquez and his family had to rely on each other for the first time. With a new plan to open yet another pharmacy—this time in Barranquilla (this would be the elder Gabriel's fifth attempt to do so)—the family, all eight, moved together to the coastal city to start fresh. This pharmacy "was not the fifth drugstore, as we used to say in the family, but the same old one that we took from city to city, depending on Papá's commercial hunches,"[27] García Márquez later joked.

García Márquez was actually very anxious about the sudden change in his life. Reuniting with his parents after years of being separated felt strange. The only family he'd known since he was a child was the strange amalgam of his grandparents and aunts in the big house in Aracataca. In fact, upon one of his first visits to his parents as a little boy, he had stood in a room filled with female relatives, wondering which one was his mother. "A lightning flash of guilt shook my body and soul because I knew that my duty was to love her but I felt that I did not,"[28] he remembered about that incident.

Nonetheless, he enrolled in school in Barranquilla, which helped set a schedule for him and provided some stability in his life. His free time was spent helping his father establish the new pharmacy. The elder Gabriel had actually sent his wife and five young children to live temporarily in Aracataca until he and Gabo could set up the pharmacy in Barranquilla. Spending time with his father proved enlightening for García Márquez. Gabriel García treated his son like a peer, showing him respect and speaking to him as he would an adult. He used anecdotes to explain his own difficult childhood, as well as his problems in school and his failed attempts to complete a degree in medicine.

The elder Gabriel was a miser, however, and was always aware of his tight budget. At one point, he decided that he and Gabo would eat only one meal a day to save money. This did not last long, as he soon caught 11-year-old Gabo surreptitiously stuffing himself with sodas and snacks.

The elder Gabriel had an appetite for reading. García Márquez refers to his father as an "absolute autodidact [one who teaches himself],"[29] who read volumes and taught himself much. In a way, such a respect for books on the elder Gabriel's part was a continuation of the influence of his father-in-law, Colonel Márquez, on young Gabo. Whereas Colonel Márquez used to relate stories of history and a love and respect of words to Gabo, Gabriel García instilled in his son a love of and fascination with learning.

That learning paid off one night, when Gabo's father left him at the house of a family friend to attend a business dinner. The family was listening to a quiz show on the radio, and the question asked was, "What animal changes its name when it rolls over?" Gabo, who had been reading the *Almanaque Bristol* that same day, knew that the answer to the perplexing question was a beetle: In Spanish, a beetle is called an *escarabajo*, but when it rolls over, it is called an *escararriba*—the suffix *abajo* means "below" and the suffix *arriba* means "above." Gabo told one of the children the answer, and she called the radio station and answered it correctly. As a result, she won 100 pesos, a substantial sum, enough to pay the family's rent for three months. The fact that the answer had come from Gabo, however, was overshadowed by the celebration that erupted, as neighbors and friends who had listened to the program rushed over to offer congratulations. When his father returned from his dinner, he also joined the celebration, unaware that his son had been the cause of it.[30]

Young García Márquez quickly showed a keen intellect and great thirst for knowledge. He was also very well balanced. He loved to read in solitude, like his father, but he also loved to be among people and to socialize, like his grandfather. Soon, it became obvious to everyone that García Márquez was truly gifted.

Finding His Calling

Although he loved to learn, García Márquez sometimes found studying difficult because, as the eldest child, he was drawn into the very real problem that his parents faced: poverty. His mother and siblings eventually moved to Barranquilla, though his father's pharmacy was barely making a profit. Young Gabo, then an adolescent, witnessed his parents' financial worries and the resulting stresses up close. He also faced the social stigma of being poor.

Trying to find ways to help his parents, García Márquez took on a series of odd jobs. He copied comic strips that appeared in local papers and sold them to people in his neighborhood. He worked at a print shop, trying to learn the trade. The owners eventually gave him a new task: standing on the street corner, handing out flyers for cough syrup. One day, he saw a woman—a family friend from Aracataca—who seemed shocked at what he was doing. Believing the work was little better than begging, she yelled at young García Márquez: "You tell Luisa Márquez to think about what her parents would say if they saw their favorite grandchild in the market handing out advertisements."[31] García Márquez did not actually repeat what the woman had said to his mother, knowing she would feel humiliated, but later recalled, "I cried into my pillow with rage and shame for several nights."[32] Months later, when his mother allowed him to leave the job, he was grateful and relieved. He had never handed out flyers again anyway. Instead, he would just throw them into the gutters.

He often resorted to lying to spare his mother's feelings. At one point, his mother, desperate for money to help feed her family, went behind her husband's back and secretly sent García Márquez to the home of a rich man who was known in Barranquilla as a generous philanthropist. He carried with him a letter, written by Luisa Márquez, begging the man for financial help on behalf of her children. "Only someone who knew her would understand what that humiliation meant in her life, but circumstances demanded it,"[33] Gabo wrote later.

However, when García Márquez went to the man's house, which was large and imposing, a woman at the door took the letter and left him waiting outside for four hours in the heat. Finally, he was told to return within a week. When he did, he was again sent away and told to come back a week later. Several more weeks went by like this, until another woman finally gave him a cold, dismissive message from the rich man: His home was not a charity. The defeated and humiliated García Márquez did not have the heart to tell his mother the news, so he roamed the streets for several hours that afternoon, thinking up a lie. He eventually went home and told her that the rich man had died, then watched in shock as his mother prayed for the man's soul. He could not bring himself to tell her the man, whom she thought was so generous, had spurned her request.

AN ACADEMIC SUCCESS

His schoolwork provided García Márquez with some relief from his family's daily financial troubles. At the age of nine, he attended the Colegio San Jose, an expensive boarding school in

Gabriel García Márquez traveled to the town of Zipaquirá, pictured here, to attend Liceo Nacional de Zipaquirá when he was 13 years old. The town is known for its Spanish colonial architecture and is approximately 16 miles north of Bogotá.

Barranquilla. He lived with a relative to save money, since his family could barely afford the school's tuition. However, they sensed his intelligence and decided to make an investment in his formal education.

He excelled at school and, when he was 13 years old, his parents sent him to the town of Zipaquirá, near the capital city of Bogotá. There, he attended the Liceo Nacional de Zipaquirá. He traveled the first part of the trip alone by ship, then had to take a train the rest of the way to Bogotá, located in Colombia's mountainous region. "That was where I felt for the first time an unknown and invisible physical state: cold,"[34] he later wrote. He slept his first night there at the home of a family friend, and remembers his shock when the sheets in his bed felt as cold as ice. The change in environment and climate made him homesick for the warm climate of the coastal region he called home, but he was determined to settle in to his new life at the school and to succeed. His parents, after all, were depending on him. After taking a placement exam, he won a national scholarship to the Liceo Nacional, which paid for his tuition and boarding. The news came as an immense relief to his parents.

García Márquez quickly made several friends, young men who came from all parts of Colombia to attend the Liceo Nacional. Because Zipaquirá was a small colonial town, there was not much to do, so García Márquez and his small circle of friends spent many hours talking and getting to know one another. "The four years of harmonious coexistence with everyone instilled a unitary vision of the nation in me," he wrote. "I discovered how diverse we were and what we were good for, and I learned and never forgot that the entire country was in fact the sum total of each one of us."[35] The students were also lucky enough to benefit from the rigorous education they received from talented teachers, who enjoyed easy friendships and long conversations with their students outside the classroom.

Professor Carlos Julio Calderón taught literature. He encouraged García Márquez's imaginative tendencies. One semester, García Márquez and his classmates were each assigned to write a story and read it aloud in class. García Márquez's story, "A Case of Obsessive Psychosis," was based loosely on some reading he had done on psychoanalyst Sigmund Freud. It received sharp criticism from his classmates for being amateurish. Professor Calderón, however, soothed García Márquez's disappointment by telling him that, although the story lacked technical skill, its theme and content were original. "He concluded that in any event I ought to continue writing even if only for my mental health," he writes. "That was the first of the long conversations we held at recreational periods and other free times during my years at the *liceo* [grammar school], to which I owe a great deal in my life as a writer."[36]

Professor Calderón's encouragement was essential to young García Márquez, who had, by now, developed a real love of literature. Like his father, he read voraciously and often read and reread favorite poems, memorizing them in order to enjoy their sound and rhythm.

Another particularly influential teacher was poet Carlos Martín. Martín treated his students with respect, holding long, intellectual discussions with them rather than hassling them about administrative issues. He trusted them to behave properly and not break any of the school's rules. He welcomed students like García Márquez to his home, where he frequently held gatherings of other poets, and he loaned García Márquez important books on poetic form and literary technique. He also helped his students start a literary center at the Liceo, as well as a newspaper.[37]

While at school, García Márquez also received an education in politics. Many of his teachers were young men who held leftist, or more liberal, political views. As a result, García Márquez "graduated with a Marxist world view,"[38] according to Jon Lee Anderson, a writer for *The New Yorker* magazine. Marxism was a popular political affiliation among many Latin American intellectuals, who were attracted to its emphasis on political, social, and economic equality.

As Jon Lee Anderson writes, García Márquez—who had always enjoyed learning about history under his grandfather's tutelage—discovered his affinity for politics at the Liceo Nacional de Zipaquirá.[39] The students there engaged in lively debates with one another and took sides with the political parties of Colombia: the Liberals and Conservatives. The Conservatives had ruled the country for many years, but by the time García Márquez was in school, the Liberal Party had gained more political ground, and the country was changing.

Although they often discussed the long-standing Conservative-Liberal rivalry, the young men at the Liceo Nacional de Zipaquirá were more interested in European politics than in the domestic affairs of Colombia. This was the early 1940s, and World War II was raging in Europe. The war was being followed closely throughout the world, even by high school boys in a small Colombian city.

Occasionally, García Márquez became tired of the grueling academic routine at the Liceo. On a vacation home, when he was close to graduating, García Márquez spent time with his younger brother, who had just been released from a correctional facility for bad behavior. While García Márquez's life was structured around his schoolwork, his brother lived happy and carefree—at least from García Márquez's perspective. The comparison was inevitable, and García Márquez began to feel frustrated with his life. He also resented the pressure that his financially strapped parents placed on him to excel. He knew that they expected him to complete his studies and become a professional—perhaps a physician or a lawyer—and then help support them financially. His mother once asked him, "Don't you realize you're the pride of the family?"[40]

García Márquez responded, in frustration, "I refuse to let you force me into being what I don't want to be or what you would like me to be."[41]

Although his family clearly wanted him to enter a profession that commanded a high salary, his mother, who recognized his creative talents, suggested to him one day, "They say that if you put your mind to it you could be a good writer."

Young García Márquez thought over her words carefully. It was the first time he had ever considered writing as a career. His initial reaction, however, was to dismiss the idea. "If you're going to be a writer," he said, "you have to be one of the great ones, and they don't make them anymore. After all, there are better ways to starve to death."[42] Little did he realize he would eventually build a very successful career in such an uncertain field.

Life in Bogotá

After graduating with his bachelor's degree from the Liceo Nacional de Zipaquirá, García Márquez reluctantly promised his parents that he would pursue a legal career. He enrolled at the law school at the Universidad Nacional de Bogotá. The law program was rigorous, but it allowed him to have his afternoons free, giving him the time to work to help pay for his expenses.

A DIFFERENT EDUCATION

The city of Bogotá, long renowned as Colombia's literary and cultural center, soon cast its spell on García Márquez, especially since his heart was not really in his legal studies in the first place. García Márquez began to frequent local cafés, where poets and writers spent their time drinking coffee and talking. These cafés and the people he met there soon changed his plans and transformed his way of thinking.

One of his favorite cafés was El Molino, which was located close to his living quarters, near the law school. The poets who went

Bogotá is Colombia's capital and South America's third-largest city, with a population of more than 7 million. After finishing college, Gabriel García Márquez spent much of his time in Bogotá listening to the intellectual and literary conversations of poets and writers in local cafés.

there were granted permanent tables because of their fame. García Márquez wrote that El Molino's owners "did not allow students a fixed table, but you could be sure of learning more and learning it better than in textbooks from the literary conversations we listened to as we huddled at nearby tables."[43] Before long, García Márquez began to miss classes now and then. This habit became more and more frequent as he realized he was receiving a better education in the cafés than in school.

Literature also began to influence García Márquez more powerfully during this time. One of his roommates, Domingo Manuel Vega, loaned him a copy of Franz Kafka's *The*

Metamorphosis. As García Márquez recalls, the book "determined a new direction for my life from its first line, which today is one of the great devices in world literature": "As Gregor Samsa awoke one morning from uneasy dreams he found himself transformed in his bed into a gigantic insect."[44] The simplicity of the writing, despite the fantastic content, lent an air of confidence and authority that fascinated García Márquez.

A PUBLISHED AUTHOR

Shortly thereafter, García Márquez sat down at a typewriter that he borrowed from Domingo Manuel Vega and began to write a short story of his own in Kafka's style. He struggled to imitate the confident voice of the master. For days, he worked on the story, editing and revising, missing class the whole time because he was so caught up in the spirit of the work. He finally finished and entitled the story "The Third Resignation," which is about a young boy who falls into a comatose state. His mother, to preserve her own emotional stability, keeps him in a coffin for eighteen years rather than allow him to die naturally. Many critics interpret the story as a comment by Márquez on the stifling rule of South American dictators over their people.

Around this time, he read an article by Eduardo Zalama Borda in the pages of *El Espectador*, the local Bogotá newspaper, that criticized the lack of creativity among the new crop of Colombian writers. García Márquez took the article as a personal challenge, and he decided to deliver a copy of his story to Borda's office.

Two weeks later, on September 13, 1947, he walked into El Molino café and was shocked to see the title of his story on the front page of the literary supplement, *Fin de Semana*, of *El Espectador*'s new issue. "My first reaction," he recalls, "was the devastating certainty that I did not have the five centavos to buy the paper. This was the most explicit symbol of my poverty."[45] He eventually got the money to buy a copy of the paper, but he was uncertain of how to handle the success.

Chilean poet Pablo Neruda became world famous as a writer of poems that linked themes of love and politics. Neruda served as a role model for Gabriel García Márquez and many other Latin American writers.

His friends read the story and congratulated García Márquez, but it was the words of a fellow law student whom he admired, Jorge Álvara Espinosa, that seemed most prophetic: "I suppose you realize the trouble you've gotten into. Now you're in the showcase of recognized writers, and there's a lot you have to do to deserve it."[46] When García Márquez expressed doubts about the story's literary merit, Espinosa added, "In any case, that story already belongs to the past.

CHILEAN POET PABLO NERUDA

Pablo Neruda, who was awarded the Nobel Prize for Literature in 1971, was a poet and politician who influenced not only Gabriel García Márquez, but also scores of other Latin American writers of his generation.

Neruda's real name was Neftalí Ricardo Reyes Basoalto, and he was born in 1904 in Chile. When he was only 13, he was already publishing articles and poems in local newspapers and journals. In 1920, he began to contribute poetry regularly to a well-known literary journal, but he adopted the pen name Pablo Neruda in honor of one of his literary influences, the Czechoslovakian poet Jan Neruda.

Neruda attended the University of Chile, where he studied French. His education and talent helped him land diplomatic jobs with the government, and he was sent to countries around the world. He became very politically astute during these years, developing a liberal political philosophy.

In 1936, shortly after the Spanish Civil War began, Neruda was devastated to learn of the murder of Federico García Lorca, the Spanish poet and dramatist, who was a personal friend. García Lorca was killed by the forces of the Spanish dictator Francisco Franco because of his leftist political views. Neruda was living in Europe at the time and protested the brutal policies of Franco, using his political connections to help Spanish refugees find homes in Chile.

In 1945, after he returned to Chile, Neruda was elected to political office. That same year, he joined the Communist Party. He began an active career of fighting for the powerless people in his country. In 1947, after he criticized the treatment of miners, he had to go underground, hiding from the government for two years. He eventually fled to Europe, where he lived and continued writing for several years.

In 1950, he published *Cantato General*, a monumental work of more than 300 poems, in which he tells the history of Latin America and emphasizes the need for social justice. Neruda died in 1973, two years after receiving the Nobel Prize. To this day, he is regarded as the finest poet from Latin America.

What matters now is the next one."[47] He offered García Márquez advice on other books he should read, as well as some words on plot, structure, and style. "I never found the courage to tell him that perhaps our conversation had determined my life,"[48] García Márquez later wrote of that moment when his first published story seemed an omen of his literary destiny.

Eduardo Zalama Borda secured a second Kafka-like story, "Eva Is Inside Her Cat," from García Márquez and published it a few weeks later, on October 25, 1947, in *El Espectador*. Borda added an editorial note that concluded, "With García Márquez, a new and notable writer has been born."[49] García Márquez was only 20 years old at the time.

Writing short stories proved to have problems of its own, especially in Colombia, where the most revered form of literary art was not fiction but poetry. For example, the popular *piedra y cielo* ("Stone and Sky") poetic movement was then at its height, and included such writers as Eduardo Carranza, Jorje Rojas, and others, who advocated a simple and direct approach to writing poetry. Another popular poet was Pablo Neruda, who connected poetry and politics. The Chilean poet, who lived in political exile for many years, was widely admired for his passionate poetry about the history of Latin America and the quest of its oppressed masses to find freedom. At the same time, he also wrote eloquent love poetry, demonstrating his versatility and range of talent.

In Colombia, as in other places in the world, literature and politics were closely linked. However, in 1948, shortly after the publication of his first set of short stories, the political situation in Colombia would explode and García Márquez would find himself immersed in it.

The year 1948 began well for García Márquez. In addition to having his short stories published in *El Espectador*, he had begun to receive recognition from the local poets and other writers for his emerging talent. Furthermore, despite his lack of interest in his law classes, he passed his courses and remained in good academic standing at the university. However, his first writing success had made its mark on him, and he began to consider a career in writing or journalism more seriously. All he knew was that, even though his parents would probably be furious with him, he was happiest not in the law class-room but in the local cafés, chatting with writers and listening to conversations about poetry, culture, and politics.

POLITICAL TURMOIL

Until this point, García Márquez had seen literature and politics as two separate realms, neither of which he understood very well. But now he was aware of the political tensions in Colombia. The Conservative Party was in control, under the presidency of Ospina Pérez, who implemented moderate policies to try to appease the country's Liberal constituents. The Liberal Party was largely fractured by many internal divisions, but with presidential elections approaching, one Liberal Party candidate was working hard to restore the party's unity.

Jorge Eliécer Gaitán was born in 1902 to poor parents. Through hard work and a reliance on his intelligence, he became a star within the Liberal Party.[50] His political philosophy was simple, but so revolutionary for the time that he is frequently referred to as the nation's "first modern politician."[51] A talented and articulate orator, he spoke to the Colombian people in an engaging manner as he explained his philosophy: the importance of their role in how they were governed. He criticized the brutal policies of the Conservative administration and its corruption. He focused on the need for the Liberal Party to resolve its internal differences. His popularity among Colombians spread quickly, and people began to feel that the nation stood on the threshold of a new beginning.

García Márquez heard one of Gaitán's speeches one night on his way home to his living quarters near the university. Gaitán spoke on a weekly basis over the public loudspeakers in Bogotá. Gaitán's words had a powerful effect on García Márquez:

That night I had the impression I was the only person on the streets. . . . To me it was a revelation, for I had allowed myself the arrogance of not believing in Gaitán, and that night I understood all at once that he had gone beyond the Spanish country and was inventing a lingua franca [a common language] for everyone, not so much because of what his words said as for the passion and shrewdness in his voice.[52]

García Márquez listened to the entire speech, which lasted more than three hours, as Gaitán spoke of the need to end political violence in Colombia and to craft a government that responded to the needs of its people. Later that night, García Márquez confessed to his roommate: "I'm a new man. . . . Now I know how and why the wars of Colonel Nicolás Márquez began."[53] By this, he meant that he understood why people like his grandfather held such intense feelings about the political events of their day, and even why people were willing to fight in wars over their political ideas.

On February 7, 1948, García Márquez attended a political march led and organized by Gaitán. It was a mock funeral march in honor of all the victims of political violence. Sixty thousand Colombians turned out for the event, wearing black and moving silently through the streets. The march marked a mass condemnation of the current government's policy of silencing its critics with violence and subjugating people to brutal polities. Gaitán's progress in his presidential campaign seemed positively destined for success, and young Gabo was excited to be part of this new, idealistic climate in Colombian politics. However, the idealism—and Gabo's sense of optimism for Colombia's future—would not last long.

A Fallen Hero

On Friday, April 9, 1948, García Márquez sat down at the dining room of the student living quarters to have lunch. Suddenly, a friend and fellow student rushed into the room, exclaiming, "They just killed Gaitán in front of El Gato Negro." In shock, García Márquez and others hurried to El Gato Negro café, which was only three blocks away from where he lived in the student dormitory. It was true: Gaitán had been shot, though not yet dead.

A group of several friends had come to Gaitán's law office and invited him to lunch to celebrate his latest legal victory. (Many think that some of these friends were actually co-conspirators in the assassination attempt, but nothing has ever been proven.) In front of the café, where Gaitán went that day without his usual cohort of bodyguards, a man shot the popular politician three times in the head. Controversy would later erupt about whether there had been one gunman or three and about how many shots had actually been fired.

Both Fidel Castro (pictured here), a young man who would later become the leader of Communist Cuba, and Gabriel García Márquez were in Bogotá the day Colombia presidential candidate Jorge Eliécer Gaitán was assassinated in 1948. A great admirer of Gaitán, Castro was scheduled to meet with him the day he was killed.

By the time García Márquez arrived on the scene, Gaitán, still clinging to life, had been taken to a local hospital, and a large pool of blood lay in front of the café's entrance. Crowds of furious people, in shock and grief, quickly sought revenge. Word spread that the assassin had been caught by the police. (This man, not named in García Márquez's memoir of the incident, was Juan Roa Sierra, whom historians agree was the sole assassin, although his motives have never been determined.) The crowds went after the man, and officers locked him away in a local drugstore, behind heavy metal gates, to protect him until they could interrogate him. The fury of the crowds overwhelmed the police, however, and they soon

JORGE ELIÉCER GAITÁN: SUPPORTER OF THE WORKING CLASS

Born in 1898 to a poor family, Jorge Eliécer Gaitán never received any formal education until he was 11 years old. His early life of poverty helped determine the issues that he would support for the rest of his life. In school, he faced social-class obstacles from classmates who came from wealthier families. Nevertheless, determined to succeed, Gaitán eventually completed a law degree in 1924 and began practicing law. He also took a teaching position at the National University of Colombia. He traveled to Rome and earned a doctorate at the Royal University.

He became politically active while he was still a student, taking part in popular demonstrations. He became recognized within the Liberal Party for his oratory skills and popular appeal, especially after the outcry against the 1928 banana workers' strike. Gaitán had some differences with the Liberal Party and started his own faction in 1933, called the Leftist Revolutionary Union. His party won support from the working and lower classes.

The Liberal Party, however, recognized that his popularity could rejuvenate its political platform and he rejoined in 1935. The next year, he became the mayor of Bogotá. In 1940, he was appointed minister of education, and helped establish major literacy programs.

Gaitán ran for president in 1946, but lost because the Liberal Party was so divided. In 1947, he became the head of the Liberal Party and sought to restore its unity, then began preparing for a second attempt at the presidency in 1948, the year he was assassinated.

released the alleged assassin to the people, who beat him to death.

García Márquez watched the scene in horror, not realizing that there was another person—a future friend—also present in the crowd. A young Cuban student named Fidel Castro had arrived in Colombia only days earlier, as a delegate from the University of Havana to attend a student conference. In fact, a great admirer of Gaitán's, Castro had had an appointment to meet with the politician later that day, a meeting that was thwarted by the assassin's bullets. Many years later, after García Márquez and Castro had become close friends, they would realize that they had both been present in front of El Gato Negro on that fateful day.[54]

The assassination of Jorge Eliécer Gaitán caused an uproar in Colombia. Liberals accused the Conservative government of being responsible for the murder, and all the old tensions between the two parties raged anew. Riots consumed the city of Bogotá and came to be known as the *Bogotazo*, or "the strike of Bogotá."[55] On a larger scale, another civil war, known as *La Violencia* (The Violence), erupted in Colombia. It would last until 1958. By the time it was over, it would be blamed for the murders of hundreds of thousands of Colombians.

On the day of Gaitán's assassination, the government office next door to the student dormitory where García Márquez lived was set on fire by rioters. The black smoke seeped into the students' rooms, and they evacuated to the streets to find the city plunged into chaos. García Márquez remembered: "Maddened hordes, armed with machetes and all kinds of tools stolen from the hardware stores, attacked and set fire to the businesses along Carrera Septima and the adjacent streets with the help of mutinous police officers."[56] In the Plaza de Bolívar, he witnessed an even more horrific sight—of dead bodies piled up, having been killed either by rioters or police officers desperately trying to maintain order. Many buildings across the city were burning, having been looted and set aflame.

García Márquez hurriedly packed a few belongings—in his haste leaving behind some manuscripts as well as the dictionary his grandfather had given him—and fled the student dormitory. He sought shelter at the home of an uncle who lived nearby with his wife and children. They all huddled in the house, afraid to go outside, and watched the city dissolve into chaos. García Márquez later wrote, "Every dream of fundamental social change for which Gaitán had died vanished in the smoking rubble of the city."[57]

It soon became obvious that the Universidad Nacional de Bogotá would not be a safe place for García Márquez to stay and continue his studies. Indeed, with the madness that had consumed the city, it was not clear if the law school would even reopen and resume classes anytime soon. The whole city seemed to have come to a halt.

García Márquez moved back to the coast, to the city of Cartagena, and enrolled at the law school of the University of Cartagena. However, life had changed dramatically for young García Márquez. He had been present for one of the most turbulent events in Colombia's modern history, and he would never think the same way again. In Cartagena, a peaceful city—as yet unscathed by La Violencia—he had some time to think and he became familiar with El Universal, the local newspaper. It had been founded only one month before García Márquez's arrival in the city by a Liberal sympathizer who hoped to change and improve the quality of Colombian journalism. García Márquez, hearing that the new editor-in-chief was seeking writers and reporters, arranged a meeting with him. García Márquez was hired to work at El Universal in his spare time from his law studies. He would work under the tutelage of Héctor Rojas Heraza, the paper's lead writer. García Márquez's column would be entitled "Period. New Paragraph," an edgy title for what the paper's editors hoped would be a popular column by an emerging young writer.

García Márquez was ambivalent about working as a journalist. What he really wanted to do was to continue writing fiction, with which he had had some success in Bogotá. At least journalism would give him a chance to write and learn the profession, so he accepted the job. Not surprisingly, he began to neglect his law studies before long and was soon spending more and more of his free time at *El Universal*'s offices.

The editor-in-chief, Clemente Manuel Zabala, a renowned writer in his own right, was impressed by García Márquez's talent and took a personal interest in him. García Márquez had many lessons to learn, however, including how to write his articles—as many as two each day—in such a way that the censor would find them acceptable. Since the outbreak of *La Violencia*, almost every newspaper and media outlet in the nation had been assigned a censor to make sure that no subversive or potentially inflammatory material was made public. The military had taken charge of the country to restore order, and censorship was one of its chief methods for maintaining control.

A NEW BEGINNING

After experiencing the upheaval in Bogotá, García Márquez decided to turn his attention to writing. While accompanying a friend to Barranquilla in September 1950, he stopped at the offices of *El Nacional* newspaper to meet some people. By the end of the night, after sharing drinks and conversation at a local café, García Márquez had become fast friends with Germán Vargas, Álvaro Cepeda Samudio, and Alfonso Fuenmayor. Together, the four men, along with some others, would come to be known as the Barranquilla Group[58]—named for the city in which they met—one that helped shape the literary and cultural direction of Colombia.

García Márquez continued to publish occasional fiction in the Bogotá newspaper *El Espectador*, but most of his time was now consumed with working on his articles for *El Universal*. In 1950, he finally decided to quit law school, which was actually just a formality since he had hardly been attending classes anyway. His decision greatly disappointed his parents, but García

(*continued on page 56*)

THE BARRANQUILLA GROUP

In 1950, when he moved to Barranquilla, Gabriel García Márquez met three young men who would go on to become huge influences in his life—both creatively and personally.

El grupo de Barranquilla, or the Barranquilla Group, as they were later dubbed, was an informal social club of young intellectuals, writers, and artists. Its members included García Márquez's friends Alfonso Fuenmayor, Germán Vargas, and Álvaro Cepeda Samudio, as well as many others. In *One Hundred Years of Solitude*, García Márquez pays tribute to these friends, and even writes himself in as a character.

García Márquez has said in interviews that the Barranquilla Group provided him with a literary education in many ways. "For me, the most important thing about the 'Barranquilla Group' is that I had all sorts of books available,"* he once said, referring to the fact that he did not read much modern literature before he met the group's members.

The informal leader of the Barranquilla Group was Ramon Vinyes, another good friend of García Márquez's. Vinyes, a well-respected local bookseller, took García Márquez and the other young members of the Barranquilla Group under his "literary wing." It was Vinyes who provided the talented young García Márquez with books and encouraged him to read some of the newest and most experimental American and British writers, such as William Faulkner, Virginia Woolf, Ernest Hemingway, and James Joyce. However, Vinyes also emphasized the importance of knowing the classical writers. García Márquez once said fondly of Vinyes:

> The old man . . . would let us get involved in all sorts of reading adventures; but he wouldn't let go of the classic anchor-line, the old guy. He'd say: 'Fine, you guys might read Faulkner, the English, Russian, or French novelists, but remember—always with ties to this.'

And he wouldn't let you do without Homer, without the Romans, he wouldn't let us run wild.**

Vinyes died in 1952, but left behind a true devotee in García Márquez. As a tribute to Vinyes, García Márquez created a character based on him in his masterpiece, *One Hundred Years of Solitude*.

At the time that he associated most closely with the Barranquilla Group, García Márquez was living in a hotel that was used as a brothel; it was all he could afford. He spent his days working on his articles and column for *El Heraldo* newspaper, and his evenings were devoted mainly to working on his fiction and reading literature. His nights were spent at the local cafés with his friends, where they would stay up often until dawn, drinking and talking about the latest in politics, social events, and literature. In these conversations, García Márquez was introduced to many interesting subjects and issues, and he learned to defend his positions and opinions on art and writing.

The Barranquilla Group, and the years that García Márquez spent in the company of its members, was so vital to his creativity that he has often struggled to explain its significance. He once said, "I've said a lot about [the Group], and it always comes out wrong; I can't manage to get it right! For me it was a time when I was completely dazzled, it's truly a discovery . . . not of literature, but of literature being applied to real life, which ultimately is the big problem of literature. Of a literature that truly matters, applied to a reality."***

* "Journey Back to the Source: An Interview with Gabriel García Márquez," *The Virginia Quarterly Review*. Translated by Gene Bell-Villada. Available online at *www.vqronline.org/viewmedia.php/prmMID/912*
** Ibid.
*** Ibid.

William Faulkner (1897–1962) was a Nobel Prize–winning writer who set most of his novels and short stories in his home state of Mississippi. Gabriel García Márquez was deeply influenced by his work and would later travel through the American South as a way to pay tribute to Faulkner.

(continued from page 53)

Márquez knew that he had to remain true to his own ambitions and pursue his talents.

Around the same time, he began work on a novel, entitled *La Casa*, about a family that very much resembled his own.[59] His inspiration for the novel was sparked during a visit to his parents, who lived in the city of Sucre, where García Márquez went to recover from a bout of pneumonia. Perhaps to help speed his recovery, his friends Vargas and Fuenmayor sent him a large crate filled with books, including novels by William Faulkner, who would be one of García Márquez's greatest literary influences. García Márquez read the books and began to imagine writing a novel of his own, based on his family's experiences and his childhood home in Aracataca.

After quitting law school, García Márquez also left his job at *El Universal* and Cartagena and moved to Barranquilla, which was, in retrospect, a fortuitous move for his creative writing career. The time he would spend with his friends helped foster his development as a fiction writer. The members of the Barranquilla Group spent many long nights in cafés, discussing the latest literary trends and debating the merits of contemporary writers.

Fuenmayor helped García Márquez land a job as a columnist at *El Heraldo*, another newspaper, where García Márquez wrote articles while continuing to work steadily on *La Casa*. However, when he finally worked up the courage to submit the manuscript to a publisher, it was rejected, greatly disappointing its author.

Around this time, García Márquez accompanied his mother to Aracataca, where she went to take care of family business related to her parents' home. García Márquez's grandparents were both deceased by this time, but the return to Aracataca set García Márquez's mind to thinking. He had been trying to understand why *La Casa* had not been successful, and he now realized that he had failed to capture his family home's spirit and allure. During a train ride, he noticed a decrepit banana plantation, with a sign announcing its name: Macondo. That name stayed in his mind.

Upon his return to Barranquilla, he began to envision an entirely new novel. Like *La Casa*, it would also be based on his own upbringing in Aracataca, but he wanted it to have a mythic spirit. He modeled the town in the novel on Aracataca, but he named it Macondo after the banana plantation he had seen on his recent trip.

In 1954, he moved back to Bogotá. The era of chaos, *La Violencia*, was winding down, and García Márquez now had an opportunity to write for *El Espectador*, the newspaper that had published his first short stories. He was struggling to earn a living at journalism, as his family had feared, and his financial situation was dire—"My poverty was absolute,"[60] he wrote of that time period. But he was happy, working on his new novel about Aracataca and writing for the same paper that had first put his name in print.

SPARKING CONTROVERSY

Later that year, García Márquez had an opportunity to travel abroad. *El Espectador* sent him on assignment to Italy to cover the news at the Vatican, where Pope Pius XII was ill and reportedly close to death (he actually survived and did not die until 1958). García Márquez decided to stay in Europe to write and travel. *El Espectador* made him a foreign correspondent, and he wrote his assigned articles and sent them to Bogotá. A year later, while he was still in Europe, his friends in the Barranquilla Group found the manuscript he had begun working on a few years earlier. The finished manuscript had been sitting in his desk drawer at the newspaper office, and his friends read it and decided to try to have it published without his knowledge. The 97-page short story came out in 1955, published as *La Hojarasca* (*Leaf Storm*). The novel did well but did not make the splash his friends thought it would.

García Márquez returned to Colombia in 1955, after *La Hojarasca*'s publication, but he became famous for another reason. The government became incensed over a story he wrote about eight Colombian sailors who had drowned near Cartagena after their ship had been caught in a storm. However, it was soon discovered that one sailor, Luis Alejandro Velasco, had miraculously survived after floating at sea without food or fresh water for more than a week. Every reporter in Colombia tried to arrange an interview with Velasco, but the Colombian Navy had ordered Velasco not to speak of his ordeal, because the incident was being investigated. Even after Velasco had recuperated and moved to his home in Bogotá, the navy kept the news quiet and dodged the press. "I was shaken by the idea that they were hiding something very serious about the catastrophe from the public," García Márquez later wrote. "More than a suspicion, today I remember it as a premonition."[61] His instinct was correct, especially as the story of Velasco and the deaths of the other sailors would soon turn García Márquez's own life upside down.

Weeks after the story broke, the staff members of *El Espectador* were able to convince Velasco to tell his story to them exclusively. García Márquez was assigned to write the story, but he accepted the task reluctantly, believing that Velasco's story would be tainted by navy propaganda or—even worse—that Velasco was milking the experience to prolong his time in the public spotlight. As a result, he told his editor that he would write the exclusive feature story, but that he would not attach his name to it—instead, he would sign Velasco's name and write the piece from a first-person point of view.

Interviewing Velasco took three weeks, and *El Espectador* published his harrowing story in 14 installments, which was later expanded to 20 due to public interest. Velasco recounted his final hours on the navy ship, which had departed from Mobile, Alabama, and was headed for the Colombian port at Cartagena. Having recently been paid back wages that were owed to them, the crew members bought several items in the United States, including large appliances, such as refrigerators, washing machines, and stoves, to bring back home with them. When they ran out of space inside the vessel, they stored the largest items outside, strapping them to the deck—a very dangerous thing to do. When the ship sailed into heavy winds, it was weighed down by the extra items and couldn't stay above water. Eight crew members who had been on deck were thrown overboard. As García Márquez documented in his article, "The primary cause of the accident was not a storm, as official sources had insisted since the beginning, but what Velasco stated in his account: an overload of domestic appliances stowed improperly on the deck of a warship."[62] Velasco also stated that the warship did not have the proper type of life rafts available for the sailors. Rather than a large life raft loaded with supplies and food, Velasco himself ended up with a small raft that had no supplies at all. It was therefore implied that, even if the other sailors had managed to get onboard one of these smaller life rafts, they still may have died, either starving to death or by having their small raft overpowered by the rough waters. The result was an embarrassing exposé of the government, which had lied to cover up the fact that its sailors had broken the rules and caused a major accident due to their irresponsibility and because they were sailing on ships that were not properly equipped.

The story, as reported in *El Espectador*, caused an unprecedented sensation in the country. Readers waited eagerly for each new installment to appear, wanting to read as much about Velasco's horrific experience—in which he ate his business card and even tried to eat his own shoes—as they did about how the government had deliberately covered up the episode's true cause. *El Espectador*'s sales and readership nearly doubled, and García Márquez could hear people in cafés, theaters, and markets throughout the city talking about the tale. Although he never signed his name to the articles, it became known that he had written each piece. As this fact leaked out and became public knowledge, García Márquez feared for his safety. Some people who were loyal to the government were angry with the damage the story was doing to its reputation. One evening, García Márquez was approached by an outraged citizen at the theater, who told him, "You are doing a disservice to the country on behalf of the Communists."[63] Another time, a reporter whose name sounded similar to García Márquez's was attacked by two men in a pub. García Márquez received an official warning from *El Espectador*'s security not to go out alone at night, because the threats against him had increased.[64]

El Espectador decided to send García Márquez out of the country for a short period of time, to cover an international conference taking place in Geneva, Switzerland. In reality, the newspaper wanted to protect him from the tension that was rising after the publication of the final installment of the story. While García Márquez was away, the government punished *El Espectador* for the bad publicity it had caused, shutting down the newspaper's offices. García Márquez was left alone in Europe, without an income or a way to get home.

8

Stranded in Europe

Being stranded in Europe, penniless and without a way to get home, García Márquez had plenty of time to think about his future.

MERCEDES

During his time abroad, García Márquez often thought about a young woman named Mercedes Barcha. García Márquez had met her years earlier when Mercedes was an adolescent. One day, when she was still a young girl, García Márquez had teased her by saying, "I'm going to marry you when you are an adult."[65] She was the daughter of a pharmacist, and her father, a Liberal under political pressure, had moved his family to Barranquilla. García Márquez had struck up a friendship with her father and spent many evenings with him in local taverns, drinking, laughing, and talking. In contrast to her youthful and animated father, Mercedes was more reserved. García Márquez wrote, "She always was amusing and amiable with me, but she had an illusionist's talent for evading questions and answers and not allowing herself to be explicit about anything."[66]

Although García Márquez had been half seriously proposing marriage to Mercedes for years, in the early 1950s, he realized he was deeply in love with the intelligent young woman. He finally asked her to attend a Sunday dance with him, and she agreed. They continued to correspond and see each other occasionally, and García Márquez's feelings only intensified. He brought up the idea of marriage, but only jokingly, to gauge her interest. Once he told her, "You should marry me because I am going to be very important."[67]

When Mercedes left to study in the city of Medellín, García Márquez missed her and came up with a plan to see her. He was in town on a journalism assignment, and a friend convinced him that he could sneak into her school and convince her to elope with him. The plan failed because García Márquez did not have the courage even to attempt it, but also because he could not talk to Mercedes, who lived under strict rules at the school. In fact, Mercedes did not even know of the plan until she read the draft of his memoir, 50 years later.[68]

Before he left for Geneva in 1955, García Márquez tried to visit Mercedes again. He passed by her home in Barranquilla and saw her "slim and distant, like a statue seated in the doorway, wearing a green dress with golden lace in that year's style, her hair cut like swallows' wings, and with the intense stillness of someone waiting for a person who will not arrive."[69] He did not speak to her, but her image stayed with him—and he was prompted to act. During a layover on his trip, he sent her a note in which he wrote, "If I do not receive an answer to this letter within a month, I will stay and live in Europe forever."[70] It was a serious declaration of his love. It was also a challenge to Mercedes to state her feelings—if she had any—for him.

A week later, in Geneva, he received a favorable reply, and he knew that Mercedes was the woman he would marry. However, his being stranded in Europe put the development of

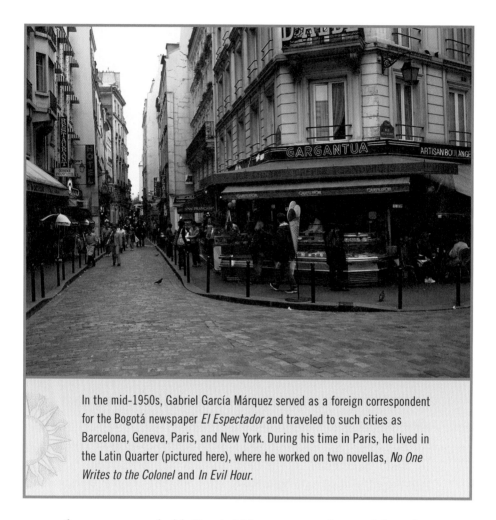

In the mid-1950s, Gabriel García Márquez served as a foreign correspondent for the Bogotá newspaper *El Espectador* and traveled to such cities as Barcelona, Geneva, Paris, and New York. During his time in Paris, he lived in the Latin Quarter (pictured here), where he worked on two novellas, *No One Writes to the Colonel* and *In Evil Hour*.

the romance on hold. García Márquez wanted to see Mercedes, but could not get back to Colombia.

WRITING STREAK

García Márquez did find a productive way to spend his time, however. While living in Europe, he worked on two new manuscripts, writing furiously day and night under the dual motivations of good ideas and plenty of free time. He lived in a small hotel in Paris's famous Latin Quarter, where the manager allowed him to put his expenses on credit. The first work he wrote was the novella *No One Writes to the Colonel*, which was about a retired colonel—probably based on his grandfather—

ERNEST HEMINGWAY

One of the greatest literary influences on Gabriel García Márquez's work was American writer Ernest Hemingway. Known as an adventurer, a journalist, and a fiction writer, Hemingway helped shape García Márquez's idea of how a writer should live.

Born in Chicago in 1899, Hemingway was a precocious child. His mother nurtured a creative spirit in him, exposing him to theater, opera, and music. His father instilled in him a love and respect of nature. As a result, Hemingway enjoyed outdoor sports, such as hunting and fishing, but also had a very refined taste for fine culture.

By the time he was an adolescent, he was already writing fiction. After he graduated from high school, he decided not to go to college and instead became a journalist. Much like García Márquez, Hemingway had no formal training in journalism. Rather, he learned the trade by writing stories and rewriting them after his editor made suggestions.

He wanted to experience more action, however, than he did covering ordinary news stories. In 1918, he signed up to be an ambulance driver for the military effort in World War I. He was sent to Italy, where he witnessed the war up close. Hemingway was injured at one point, shot in the leg, and it took him months to recover.

After the war, he began working on a novel. Over the next few years, he continued to travel, covering various international events. He also published several wildly successful novels, including *The Sun Also Rises*, *For Whom the Bell Tolls*, and *The Old Man and the Sea*.

Hemingway was politically vocal, and he owned a home in Havana at the time of Fidel Castro's Communist revolution. Hemingway publicly declared his support for Castro. In 1954, he was awarded the Nobel Prize for Literature. However, he developed a habit of drinking heavily, and in 1961, he committed suicide.

Like William Faulkner, Ernest Hemingway (1899–1961) played a significant role in helping to mold Gabriel García Márquez's work. In his novella *No One Writes to the Colonel*, García Márquez patterned his writing style after Hemingway's simple, straightforward, and deeply powerful prose, which helped Hemingway win the Nobel Prize for Literature in 1954.

who is honorable, proud, gallant, and idealistic. Struggling with poverty, he waits in vain for the pension check owed to him by the military to arrive.

The novella consumed García Márquez. "He worked day and night in a real fury," writes Mario Vargas Llosa, and one day his typewriter broke down. He took it to a repair shop, where the repairman, scratching his head, offered his diagnosis of the problem with pity in his voice: "It is exhausted, sir!"[71]

As he had done in *Leaf Storm*, García Márquez tried to recreate Aracataca and its mystique in *No One Writes to the Colonel*, but felt that he had failed again. The town he created in this novella had no name. He put the manuscript away, considering it unworthy of publication.

Despite his personal frustration with the manuscript, one can trace the development of García Márquez's writing style from *Leaf Storm* to *No One Writes to the Colonel*. Although *Leaf Storm* was deeply influenced by the work of William Faulkner—of whose work García Márquez greatly admired—in *No One Writes to the Colonel*, Faulkner's influence had disappeared, giving way to that of another great writer, Ernest Hemingway. A famous American writer and adventurer, and author of such novels as *The Sun Also Rises* and *For Whom the Bell Tolls*, Hemingway was known for his simple, straightforward, but deeply powerful writing style, which also defines García Márquez's *No One Writes to the Colonel*.

During his time in Europe, García Márquez also worked on a second novella: *In Evil Hour*, about a town struggling under government oppression and violence—similar to *La Violencia*. The work involves many of the same characters who appeared in *No One Writes to the Colonel*. The towns in both novellas were modeled after Aracataca, but García Márquez still felt that he had not captured his hometown's spirit.

García Márquez also made use of his free time by traveling as much as possible on his very limited budget. He still managed to tour East Germany, Czechoslovakia, Poland, Russia, and Hungary[72] during 1957, and he worked as a freelance journalist during that time. However, he missed Colombia, his friends, and Mercedes terribly, and as he traveled, he wondered how long it would be before he would see them again.

9

The Cuban Revolution

In 1957, after nearly three years of surviving alone in Europe, García Márquez was able to save up enough money to return to Colombia. In 1958, he married Mercedes Barcha, who had waited loyally for him. The newlyweds moved to Venezuela, where, in the city of Caracas, García Márquez wrote for the newspaper *Momento*. In 1959, an event took place that would have a major impact on García Márquez's life and career: the Cuban Revolution. On the island of Cuba, Fidel Castro had overthrown the dictator Fulgencio Batista and established a Communist government.

COMMUNIST SYMPATHIES

García Márquez, who had always been a supporter of Communism, was happy and pleased by the Cuban Revolution. During *La Violencia*'s early days, when he was still a law student, he had attended underground meetings of the Colombian Communist Party, a group he considered "the comrades who were the first colonizers of my

Cuban rebel soldiers, such as the ones pictured on this tank at the University of Havana, helped overthrow Cuban dictator Fulgencio Batista, who fled to the Dominican Republic on January 1, 1959. Shortly thereafter, Fidel Castro took control of the country and made Cuba the first Communist state in the Western Hemisphere.

political conscience."[73] Although he did not continue to attend meetings, perhaps realizing that he could better serve the group by focusing on his studies, he did maintain his sympathy for the Communist cause. During the three years he spent in Europe, he traveled to Russia, which was then under a Soviet (Communist) government, and later wrote: "My definitive impression is that the Soviet phenomenon—from its most unusual aspects to the simplest ones—is so complex that it cannot be reduced to propagandistic formulas, neither capitalist nor communist."[74]

After Fidel Castro took over the Cuban government, García Márquez—then employed by *Momento*—was one of

FIDEL CASTRO AND CUBA

Fidel Castro was born in Cuba in 1926. He studied to be a lawyer and was politically active. Castro supported Marxism as a governmental philosophy and was opposed to the dictatorial regime in Cuba. In 1953, he attempted to lead a revolt against Fulgencio Batista, the Cuban dictator. The revolution failed, and Batista's regime exiled Castro from the island. Ever resourceful, Castro organized a small battalion of 81 men and reentered Cuba in 1956. After a three-year struggle, he overthrew Batista and became the leader of Cuba. The success of his revolution stunned the world, winning Castro the admiration of many people in Latin America, but the hostility of many others in the United States and Europe, who preferred democracy to Marxism.

Problems between the United States and Cuba began almost immediately and came to a head in 1962, when the United States learned of a Soviet plot to install nuclear weapons sites on the Caribbean island. Under orders from President John F. Kennedy, the Americans enforced a blockade around Cuba to prevent Soviet ships from delivering supplies to the island. For 13 days, the world stood on the brink of nuclear war. The Cuban Missile Crisis, as the incident became known, was finally settled peacefully, although tensions remain between Cuba and the United States to this day.

Establishing Cuba as a socialist state, Castro instituted many broad reforms. Soon, however, his regime's mistreatment of political critics and opponents caused many to grow disillusioned with his rule. One of the few supporters he has among Latin American intellectuals is García Márquez, who met him in 1975 and has been his close friend ever since.

the first reporters to arrive in Havana to cover the new regime. In 1960, he returned to Bogotá from Venezuela and worked for *Prensa Latina*, the news agency founded by the Cuban revolutionary command. García Márquez opened the Bogotá office and ran it with his close friend, journalist Plinio Apuleyo Mendoza, with whom he had toured Russia a few years earlier.

In 1961, *Prensa Latina* moved García Márquez to the United States to work as its foreign correspondent there. He moved with Mercedes to New York, took up residence in a Manhattan apartment, and continued to cover the news. The headline story at the time was the rising tension between the United States and Cuba. John F. Kennedy had recently been elected president of the United States, and the U.S. government was working to overthrow Castro's regime and restore the former Cuban government. The disastrous Bay of Pigs invasion took place in the spring of 1961. During this failed operation, Cuban exiles, trained by the United States, attempted an attack on Cuba. They were supposed to receive military aid, especially in the form of air cover, from the U.S. military, but this aid never materialized and the mission failed, causing great embarrassment to the Kennedy administration. García Márquez covered the event and was critical of the United States.

Living in the United States was not easy, but García Márquez and Mercedes made do. Earlier that year, Mercedes had given birth to the couple's first child, a son named Rodrigo. García Márquez, overjoyed, also worked steadily at revising *In Evil Hour*, the novella he had begun in Paris. However, after the failed Bay of Pigs attack, many changes occurred within Fidel Castro's Cuban government. The administration cracked down on dissent within its borders, and many felt that free speech was being stifled. The director of *Prensa Latina*, Jorge Ricardo Masetti, whom García Márquez liked and respected, resigned, and out of a sense of solidarity, García Márquez resigned also.

His resignation was a hasty move. He had only been in New York for a few months and now had a young son, as well as a wife, to support. He decided to return to Latin America, but via a more scenic route. He, Mercedes, and Rodrigo took a

WILLIAM FAULKNER

Gabriel García Márquez has never made a secret of the immense debt he feels he owes to the American novelist William Faulkner. When he read Faulkner's work, set in Mississippi, he saw "affinities of all kinds . . . between the cultures of the Deep South and the Caribbean."*

Faulkner was born in 1897 near Oxford, Mississippi, and his experiences were quite similar to García Márquez's. His great-grandfather was a colonel during the American Civil War. His maternal grandmother, a dynamic and imaginative woman, lived with his family. As a young man, Faulkner dropped out of high school and served briefly in the military, then drifted from job to job. Unhappy in all the places he worked, he wrote poetry and read as much as possible.

In 1925, he moved to New Orleans, Louisiana, where he became part of a literary circle that included writer Sherwood Anderson. His first novel was published in 1926. Faulkner's work focused on a region of the Deep South that he named Yoknapatawpha County, a fictionalized place based on his childhood home. Faulkner was a talented experimentalist who played with the narrative structure of his fiction. In 1929, he published *The Sound and the Fury*, a psychological novel told by four different narrators.

Faulkner, who won the Nobel Prize in 1950, was well regarded abroad as well as in the United States. His novels were widely translated and he was very popular among Latin American readers like García Márquez, who appreciated Faulkner's sense of place and innovative narrative style.

* Gabriel García Márquez, *Living to Tell the Tale*. Edith Grossman, trans. (New York: Vintage Books, 2004), 404.

bus through the American South in a trip that García Márquez considered a tribute to William Faulkner, who lived in and wrote about that region of the United States.

In the 1960s, the American South was torn by racial strife and tension. The civil rights movement to fight for racial equality was under way, and segregation—a decades-old institution in the Deep South—was under attack as immoral and unjust. The backlash against those who were trying to overturn the old, racist norms was severe: Lynching, beatings, and riots were commonplace. The racism was not just directed against African Americans. As Latin Americans, García Márquez and Mercedes also witnessed ethnic discrimination as well as ignorance about Hispanic culture, such as signs in public places that declared, "No dogs or Mexicans allowed."[75]

After they reached New Orleans, Louisiana, the family ran out of money. García Márquez had to contact his friend, fellow journalist Plinio Apuleyo Mendoza, to wire him enough money to get to Mexico, where García Márquez would spend many creative years.

A NEW HOME

The family arrived in Mexico City and, as García Márquez says often, they "never really left."[76] Mexico provided a safe haven for García Márquez, who had not enjoyed his brief stint in the United States at all. In fact, as a journalist working for the Communist Cuban *Prensa Latina*, he had received angry letters and even death threats from anti-Communist Americans. After he left the United States in 1961, he was placed on a blacklist of people who would be denied entry into the United States in the future (this ban on García Márquez was enforced until 1971).[77]

García Márquez and his wife enjoyed living in Mexico City, which was a place where art and culture flourished, free from the political tumult that made life in Colombia so difficult. Always disciplined and focused, García Márquez quickly found work to support his family by working in the Mexican film industry. He worked on screenplays and wrote subtitles for films, making enough money to pay the family's expenses while also saving time for himself to write creatively.

In 1961, the same year that he landed in Mexico, his novel *No One Writes to the Colonel* was finally published. Although García Márquez had initially considered it a failure, the novella received very positive reviews from the literary community. The story of its publication is yet another testament to the loyalty and support of his friends. García Márquez had originally hidden the manuscript in a suitcase in Colombia and forgotten about it. Just as they had done with *Leaf Storm*, the Barranquilla Group's members found it and sent it to a publisher. Thus, the book was "rescued from moth-eaten oblivion by his friends,"[78] as one biographer puts it.

During the next year, 1962, a collection of García Márquez's short stories was published. Entitled *Big Mama's Funeral*, it did not receive much attention, but the critics received it favorably. Encouraged, García Márquez kept writing, logging many hours at his typewriter. He continued to revise the second manuscript he had started writing while in Paris, *In Evil Hour*. Also in 1962, his second child—another son, Gonzalo—was born.

The Barranquilla Group contacted García Márquez in 1962 and told him about the Colombian national novel contest in Bogotá. The prize for the best fiction manuscript was publication, and, as his friend Guillermo Angulo told him, the winner also received a monetary prize of 15,000 pesos. His friends encouraged him to enter some of his work. García Márquez finished and revised *In Evil Hour* and mailed it to Angulo, securing the manuscript's pages with a necktie. Angulo then forwarded it to the contest committee.

To García Márquez's immense gratification, he learned that his novel had won first place in the contest. However, its publication later that same year proved to be a great embarrassment to him. The prize committee had sent *In Evil Hour* to a Spanish publishing company in Madrid. The editors there took many liberties with the language of the novel, stripping it of its Colombian dialect and flavor and converting it to standard, formal Spanish. They also edited and, in some cases, even deleted entire scenes that they deemed improper or questionable. The result devastated García Márquez. The voice of his novel, which he had struggled to perfect, was altered beyond recognition. His characters lacked any local flavor in their language. Even worse, the copy of the manuscript he had submitted was the only one he had, so he would have to rewrite it almost from scratch to recapture the original work. Upset and angry, García Márquez decided to officially disconnect himself from the work, refusing to be associated with its publication.

Several years later, when the novella's original language was restored and *In Evil Hour* republished, it included a note from the author: "In 1962, when *La mala hora* was first published, a copy-editor gave himself permission to change certain terms and to stiffen the style in the name of the purity of the language. On this occasion, the author in his turn has given himself permission to restore the idiomatic inaccuracies and stylistic barbarisms, in the name of his sovereign and arbitrary will."[79] The episode of the novel's publication, in the end, demonstrates García Márquez's total dedication to the purity of his work and his devotion to his creative vision as a writer.

The experience, however, hurt him personally. For the next three years, despite encouragement from his friends and his wife, García Márquez did not work seriously on his fiction. He did continue to write subtitles for films and even cowrote a screenplay, but his creative spark had been diminished by the negative experience of *In Evil Hour*'s publication, as well as by the fact that none of his published books thus far had sold well or earned him fame. Most of all, he still felt like he had failed to recreate the experience of Aracataca, despite his attempts to do so in several works of fiction. He was almost ready to give up on this endeavor and he began to question his talent as a fiction writer.

10

Writing the Masterpiece

A VISION OF MACONDO

A family vacation to Acapulco, Mexico, in 1965, proved to be García Márquez's creative saving grace. During the car ride from Mexico City, he suddenly had a very clear and distinct vision of how a novel on Aracataca should be structured. He has never been able to explain the epiphany very clearly. "All of a sudden—I don't know why—I had this illumination on how to write the book.... I had it so completely formed that right there I could have dictated the first chapter word by word to a typist,"[80] he later recalled. He was so moved by this vision and so eager to get started writing that he immediately canceled the trip, startling his family, and headed back to Mexico City.

There, he informed Mercedes and his bewildered children that he would be spending at least the next six months in his office in the house, working on the manuscript of a new novel. That is exactly what he proceeded to do: He locked himself in his office with his

Throughout his writing career, Gabriel García Márquez had worked to find a way to accurately capture the spirit of his hometown, Aracataca. He finally succeeded in his novel *One Hundred Years of Solitude*, published in 1967.

typewriter and a supply of paper and cigarettes. The family was not allowed to disturb him, and Mercedes was given the task of keeping his friends and any other visitors from interrupting him. All household decisions—from the family finances to the rearing of their two children—became Mercedes's sole responsibility. Luckily for García Márquez, he had married a woman who knew his talent; she understood the urgency of his need to write, and she did everything in her power to protect his solitude.

Over the years, there has been much speculation about what rekindled García Márquez's urge to write, and what sparked his vision of yet another novel based on Aracataca. He tried to explain it once, saying:

> The tone that I eventually used in *One Hundred Years of Solitude* was based on the way my grandmother used to tell stories. She told things that sounded supernatural and fantastic, but she told them with complete naturalness. What was most important was the expression she had on her face. She did not change her expression at all when telling her stories and everyone was surprised. In previous attempts to write, I tried to tell the story without believing in it. I discovered that what I had to do was believe in them myself and write them with the same expression with which my grandmother told them: with a brick face.[81]

What García Márquez had finally discovered—after several years of trying to write the novel based on Aracataca—was the *voice* of Aracataca. To his surprise, it was the voice of his maternal grandmother, Tranquilina Márquez, whose stories had fueled his imagination since he was a young boy.

García Márquez attacked the challenge of writing his novel with gusto and enthusiasm. Every day, he wrote for several hours, and he only rarely came out of his office. The writing took much longer than he or his family anticipated—three times as long, in fact: He spent not 6 months, but 18 months, on the novel. In the meantime, because he refused to work on screenplays or any other writing, García Márquez was not earning any money. Desperate for funds, Mercedes sold almost every appliance, including her hair dryer, that the family owned. The family car was also sacrificed for the sake of the new novel.

Luckily, García Márquez's friends helped out. "His friends started to call his smoke-filled room 'The Cave of the Mafia,'" writes one biographer, "and after a while the whole community began helping out, as if they collectively understood that he was creating something remarkable."[82] Local business owners allowed Mercedes to buy items on credit, and neighbors let her borrow appliances and supplies that she needed.[83] The family was almost $10,000 in debt when García Márquez finally emerged from his office 18 months later with a 1,300-page manuscript in hand.

He was not sure what the critical reception of the novel would be, but he had reason to believe it would be positive. One year into his writing frenzy, he had sent the first few chapters to a fellow writer, the well-respected Carlos Fuentes (with whom García Márquez had coauthored a screenplay). Fuentes spread the word that García Márquez was working on an excellent book. He wrote in a magazine, "I have just read eighty pages from a master."[84] García Márquez even allowed brief excerpts to be published in literary journals and magazines, which also helped build anticipation about the novel.

SUCCESS AT LAST

After borrowing money for postage, García Márquez mailed the manuscript to the Editorial Sudamericana publishing company in Buenos Aires, Argentina. The novel was quickly accepted by the editors, and it appeared in print in 1967. The first print run—8,000 copies—sold out in only one week. The publisher could barely keep up with the public's demand for *One Hundred Years of Solitude*. The copies sold out almost every week for the next several months. Within the first three years after its publication, half a million copies had been sold.

The success hardly stopped there. Translations of the novel were quickly commissioned, and the international literary community soon had the opportunity to appreciate García Márquez's talent as well. In 1969, *One Hundred Years of Solitude* won the Chianchiano Prize in Italy and was named the Best Foreign Book in France. In 1970, literary critics in the United States, where a ban was technically still in effect on García Márquez, selected the novel as one of the 12 best books

Gabriel García Márquez's childhood home (pictured here) in Aracataca, Colombia, was designated a national monument after he won the Nobel Prize in 1982. Local leaders plan to make Aracataca a tourist destination by turning García Márquez's home into a museum and building a park in his honor.

of the year.[85] The novel continued to garner several national and international prizes over the next several years, and it was eventually translated into more than 30 languages.

What made *One Hundred Years of Solitude* such a wildly successful novel and its author an overnight celebrity? Several factors contributed to its popularity and critical acclaim.

First, the novel has a distinctive voice. *One Hundred Years of Solitude* is a fantastic novel, in which unimaginable events take place as if they were common occurrences: A young woman eats dirt while another ascends into the sky, carried away by a windstorm; one man is followed around by clouds of butterflies while another tinkers away, creating small fish shapes out of metal; people live to be hundreds of years old, while others die and are resurrected. These events are related in

ARACATACA TODAY

Macondo, the fictional village that García Márquez immortalized in *One Hundred Years of Solitude*, was based on the beloved village of his childhood: Aracataca. Originally home to several banana plantations, Aracataca was already sliding into economic decline by the time García Márquez was born. The town has never recovered from the sudden pull-out of the United Fruit Company. Furthermore, the political problems that have plagued Colombia in the past several years have hit Aracataca's 15,000 citizens especially hard: One-third of the residents are unemployed, many have been killed during conflicts with guerrillas, and García Márquez himself has not visited since the early 1980s for fear that he will be kidnapped by guerrillas.

However, in the last couple of years, the Colombian government and the local Aracataca authorities have made plans to revive the town by paying tribute to its most famous former resident. "We don't have any oil here, and we don't have any gold mines," says the town's secretary of social development. "The only mine that we have is the exploitation of Gabo."*

Rafael Dario Jimenez, director of the García Márquez home museum, is working on a plan with town officials to rebuild the house. They also want to restore some of the town's historic buildings and establish a resource center for people studying García Márquez's life and work. They have already started to build a park dedicated to García Márquez, complete with a sculpture garden in which readings and cultural events will take place. All this effort, they hope, may rejuvenate Aracataca's economy by attracting tourists and restoring the glory of the village.

* Gary Marx, "Locals Aim to Transform Nobel Writer's Town into Tourist Destination," *Chicago Tribune*, September 25, 2005. Available online at *www.duluthnewstribune.com*.

a matter-of-fact, confident voice. As Mario Vargas Llosa writes, "Fantasy has broken its chains and gallops wild and feverish, permitting itself all excesses."[86] Second, the novel finally accomplishes García Márquez's goal of depicting the Aracataca of his childhood. In *One Hundred Years of Solitude*, the small village where he grew up is called Macondo. The novel spans a century in the history of the village, beginning with its establishment, and traces the lives of its founders, the Buendía family. García Márquez documents the history of Macondo by describing the lives of the members of the Buendía clan. The Macondo that emerges is one of mythic proportions.

Third, *One Hundred Years of Solitude* incorporates much of Colombia's history and politics into its storyline. Thus, the story of Macondo can be interpreted as a representation of the overall history of Colombia as a nation. According to literary critic Regina James, "García Márquez once remarked that the reader of *Cien años de soledad* who was not familiar with the history of his country, Colombia, might appreciate the novel as a good novel, but much of what happens in it would make no sense to him."[87] One of the events García Márquez depicts in the novel is the famous banana workers' strike of 1928, about which his grandfather Colonel Nicolás Márquez had told him about many years before. Of course, García Márquez fictionalizes some aspects of these historical events. For example, in depicting the banana strike, in which hundreds of people were killed, García Márquez increases the number of casualties to thousands for dramatic effect.

García Márquez also writes about his personal history in *One Hundred Years of Solitude*, and he creates characters based on—and often directly named after—his family and friends. Other characters are clearly intended to represent his grandfather and grandmother. In many ways, *One Hundred Years of Solitude* serves as a testament to all that is and ever was important to García Márquez, from his childhood until the time he wrote the novel, when he was not yet 40 years old.

Politics and the Nobel Prize

The celebrity he gained with the publication of *One Hundred Years of Solitude* overwhelmed García Márquez. It seemed that every newspaper, magazine, radio station, and media outlet wanted to interview him, to question, learn from, and understand him. In 1971, Peruvian novelist and critic Mario Vargas Llosa published *Gabriel García Márquez: The Story of a Deicide*, a biography and analysis of García Márquez's work (a "deicide" is the act of killing a divine being or god). Many similar books would follow, as García Márquez's reputation as one of the world's greatest novelists was cemented. *Leaf Storm, No One Writes to the Colonel, In Evil Hour,* and *Big Mama's Funeral*, which had hardly received any attention at the time of their original publication, were now reissued in new editions and sold very well.

A QUIET CELEBRITY

Ironically, the attention García Márquez received made him want to retreat from the world. Shortly after the publication of *One Hundred*

The success of *One Hundred Years of Solitude*, which was translated into English in 1970, sparked an increased interest in Gabriel García Márquez's other work. Suddenly, bookstores throughout the world were filled with titles he had written.

Years of Solitude, he was invited to Buenos Aires, Argentina, to judge a fiction competition. In the city, he attended the theater one evening, and when he walked in, he was surprised to find his arrival being announced. He was introduced to the crowd as the author of *One Hundred Years of Solitude* and the crowd spontaneously gave him a standing ovation.[88] He responded to his astonishing, newfound fame in his usual, disciplined way—

by focusing on his next writing project. It was a short story collection entitled *Innocent Eréndira and Other Stories*, which was published in 1972. A year later, he published *When I Was Happy and Uninformed*, a book that collected his many major journalistic writings of the past 20 years.[89]

In 1975, he published his sixth work of fiction, *Autumn of the Patriarch*, about a Latin American dictator. The novel illuminates the corrupting influence of power and the necessary solitude forced on anyone who holds it. It also emphasizes the destruction and ruin that can befall a nation when all its power is in the hands of one person. What is amazing about the novel, perhaps more than its content, is its format: The novel is written in a stream of lengthy, unpunctuated sentences that flow together, representing the narrator's memories of the dictator's long rule. Allen Ruch, a writer and founder of *www.themodernword.com*, an award-winning Web site dedicated to the work of writers such as García Márquez, notes that the book's "dense but fluid prose . . . makes *Autumn of the Patriarch* García Márquez's most challenging novel; but it also makes it one of his most exciting."[90] Upon its publication, García Márquez was praised for creating an innovative, though risky, structure.

The protagonist, the dictator, is an amalgam of many different world dictators, including Augusto Pinochet of Chile, Rafael Trujillo of the Dominican Republic, Rojas Pinilla of Colombia, and Francisco Franco of Spain. García Márquez said, "My intention was always to make a synthesis of all the Latin American dictators, but especially those from the Caribbean,"[91] although the Soviet Union's Joseph Stalin was also a model.

García Márquez had always been intrigued by power and especially by the way it was wielded by dictators. This interest dated back to 1957, when he was living in Venezuela, having recently returned from his exile in Paris. As a journalist in Caracas, he covered a military coup that overthrew the country's dictator.

García Márquez stood with other reporters outside the room where the military's top officials were debating which one of them should be the country's next leader. "I was just there like all the others, covering the news and hoping the meeting would end quickly so I could go home and go to sleep," García Márquez said. "Suddenly the door opened and a general came out walking backward, his gun drawn and pointing into the room, his boots covered with mud."[92] He left the building, his gun pointed at the room the entire time; clearly, he was afraid he would be assassinated in the "voting" process. After he fled, the officials in the room quickly arrived at their decision on the new leader. The violent and impulsive way in which power was decided and leaders were chosen made an impact on the young journalist.

SUPPORT FOR FIDEL CASTRO

By the late 1970s, García Márquez had moved back to Bogotá, Colombia, although he was still spending a lot of time in Mexico City. He used some of the money he was now making to start a news magazine, *Alternativa*, which had a leftist political and social perspective.[93] His views on Cuba and Communism were now well known. In 1977, he published a book entitled *Operation Carlota*. It was a collection of political essays on Cuba, specifically relating to its role in Angola, Africa. In 1975, Angola, which had been a colony of Portugal, finally became an independent nation. However, political forces within the country began vying for power. Backed by the Cuban military, one political party seized power and established a Marxist government. Cuba was widely criticized for its actions, and García Márquez's *Operation Carlota* was seen as propaganda in support of Fidel Castro.

In 1980, García Márquez helped secure the release of Cuban poet Heberto Padilla, whose case had been causing controversy since 1971. That year, the poet had been arrested by Fidel Castro's government and imprisoned for counterrevolutionary activity. Writers and intellectuals throughout Latin America

Although many people claimed that Cuban leader Fidel Castro was using his relationship with Gabriel García Márquez for his own gain, García Márquez ignored the public outcry and maintained a close friendship with Castro. The two are pictured here having dinner in 2000.

were outraged and sent a petition of protest to Castro. The fact that freedom of speech seemed to be under attack in Cuba angered many people, especially those who had originally supported Castro's Communist revolution. Many of those former supporters had grown disillusioned over the years—except for García Márquez, who still held a positive view of the revolution and of Castro's policies.

During the time of Padilla's arrest in 1971, García Márquez was traveling abroad, so one of his colleagues added his name to the petition, assuming that would be acceptable to García Márquez. However, his colleague's assumption angered García Márquez. He had not wanted his name added to the petition at all. Later, when Padilla was released but forced to "confess" to his alleged crimes against the government, a second letter from the intellectuals protesting this treatment did not include García Márquez's signature. Many people were puzzled over this discrepancy, but later realized that García Márquez actually admired Fidel Castro. In fact, when García Márquez traveled to Cuba in 1975, he met and became a close friend of the controversial leader.

His friendship with the Cuban leader drew criticism from many of his colleagues in the literary community. García Márquez replied to the criticism by saying that he had access to "much better and more direct information, and a political maturity that allows me a more serene, patient, and humane comprehension of the reality."[94]

Despite his words, his colleagues felt that García Márquez had actually become blinded by Castro's influence and was allowing the Cuban leader to use him as a public relations pawn. In the 1970s and 1980s, pictures of the two together appeared frequently in the media, reinforcing their public friendship. Indeed, Castro even gave García Márquez a house in Havana, where García Márquez stayed during visits to the island-nation.

However, in 1980, García Márquez made good use of his friendship. He convinced Castro to allow Padilla, who was still being closely monitored by the government, to leave Cuba. Padilla's release was positively received, but critics continued to point out to García Márquez that many more political prisoners were still languishing in Castro's prisons. In response, García Márquez later publicly lamented, "There are more than 2,000 former political prisoners . . . that I helped to set free and I did it quietly. Sometimes they didn't even ask me to do it or they didn't know about my interceding. Some of them, once freed, have turned against me."[95] Nonetheless, García Márquez refused to criticize Castro, a position that made things very difficult for him personally.

In 1981, García Márquez ran into problems with the Colombian government again. By this time, pro-Communist groups, with which García Márquez, as a socialist, sympathized, had declared a revolution against the government. Shortly after García Márquez had returned from a trip to visit Fidel Castro in Cuba, the Colombian military accused the novelist of helping to support the antigovernment guerrilla groups. Learning that he would soon be arrested, García Márquez (and Mercedes) were forced to seek asylum at the Mexican Embassy in Bogotá. From there, they were able to fly out of the country and back to Mexico.

Because of García Márquez's celebrity as the Spanish-speaking world's leading novelist, the story of his escape and the conflict with the Colombian government made headlines throughout the world. He was invited to France, where the French government awarded him the French Legion of Honor, the most prestigious decoration that France awards to a non-French person.[96] Other governments also expressed their support of García Márquez. Because of his shaky relationship with the Colombian government, however, he resettled his family in Mexico City.

Later in 1981, he published *Chronicle of a Death Foretold*, a novel that, like *One Hundred Years of Solitude*, was set in a small town on the Colombian coast. García Márquez experimented once again with form, taking creative liberties with the narrative. In the novel, the death of the main character, Santiago Nasar, is told many times, from different perspectives, by various characters before the actual death takes place. The novel was a critical success. But García Márquez's biggest recognition was yet to come.

WINNING THE NOBEL PRIZE

In 1982, Gabriel García Márquez was at his home in Mexico City when the phone rang early one morning. He answered it, and was shocked to hear that it was the Swedish Academy, awarding him that year's Nobel Prize for Literature. The Academy had selected him for "his novels and short stories, in which the fantastic and the realistic are combined in a richly composed world of imagination, reflecting a continent's life

Gabriel García Márquez won the Nobel Prize for Literature in 1982. He is pictured here with Swedish king Carl XVI Gustaf, who annually presents the award at the Nobel Prize ceremony in Stockholm, Sweden.

and conflicts."[97] The Academy also noted García Márquez's political leanings: "Like most of the other important writers in the Latin American world, García Márquez is strongly committed, politically, on the side of the poor and the weak against domestic oppression and foreign economic exploitation."[98]

His friends recalled his surprise at winning the literary community's most prestigious award. "I got a call from Spain at about 4 A.M. that Gabo had been awarded the Nobel Prize," said his friend Maroa Luisa Eli. "I put on a pair of pants and a sweater and left for his house, and there was Mercedes with all the phones off the hook. There was a big sign on the door of their house that said 'Congratulations.' He had these big eyes wide open as if he were hallucinating."[99] Another friend had gone to Mexico City to visit García Márquez, and he happened to arrive the same day García Márquez won the Nobel Prize. Unaware of the award, the friend saw that the house was filled with flowers and assumed that García Márquez had died![100]

The presentation of the Nobel Prize to a South American writer was a victory not just for García Márquez but for the Spanish-speaking world in general. The new Colombian president, Belisario Betancur, quickly moved to restore the country's relationship with its internationally renowned native son. He personally promised García Márquez protection and invited him to move back to Colombia. García Márquez did return, but he maintained his other homes in Mexico City and Havana.

For his next writing project, García Márquez once again turned to his family's rich and intriguing past. In 1985, he published *Love in the Time of Cholera*, a romance based on the difficult courtship between his parents. Set in a small Caribbean port city, much like Cartagena, the novel traces the love between two characters, Florentino Ariza and Fermina Daza. Ariza pines for Daza, his first love, for decades, even though she is married to another man. He attempts to renew their passion after the death of her husband. On the night of his rival's funeral, Ariza declares his feelings for Daza, and the two, now much older, rekindle their love. The theme of suffering for love was not one that García Márquez had previously written about, but the novel became one of his most popular books.

THE NOBEL SPEECH

When he won the Nobel Prize for Literature in 1982, Gabriel García Márquez delivered a powerful lecture. In his speech, entitled "The Solitude of Latin America," García Márquez focused on several issues that were close to his heart, especially the literary tradition and the political situation in his home region.

He criticized Europeans for failing to understand both Latin America's problems and its attempts to change its political and social systems. Offering a series of staggering statistics about the violence and poverty in the region, he noted, "There have been five wars and seventeen military coups. . . . [T]wenty million Latin American children died before the age of one—more than have been born in Europe since 1970."

However, he cited the decades of struggle as a source of the creativity of the region's most exalted writers, including himself. "We have had to ask but little of imagination," he said, because their everyday lives are filled with unbelievable—mostly tragic—events. He challenged European society to understand—not criticize—the tumult in Latin America, and reminded Europe of its own history of wars. He also asked that the recognition of a Latin American writer not be viewed as an unusual phenomenon. His success as a writer, he implied, is inseparable from the everyday experiences of life in his homeland.

The "solitude" of Latin America, he said, is a result of the fact that European society views its problems as unsolvable. Yet, he insisted, the very fact that he and other writers are expressing the hope of social change is one reason to expect a better future. As he said, "Why is the originality so readily granted us in literature so mistrustfully denied us in our difficult attempts at social change?"*

* Gabriel García Márquez, "The Solitude of Latin America." Available online at *http://www.nobelprize.org/literature/laureates/1982/marquez-lecture-e.html*

Today, Gabriel García Márquez continues to keep a strict writing routine, even as he travels between his various homes around the world. In addition to writing, he purchased the Colombian news magazine *Cambio* in 1999 and serves as the publication's editorial board director and main reporter.

García Márquez's writing during the 1990s consisted of more fiction as well as journalistic articles. In 1990, he published *The General in His Labyrinth*, another historical novel. It was about Simón Bolívar, who had been García Márquez's hero as well as the hero of his grandfather, Colonel Nicolás Márquez. In the novel, García Márquez humanizes Bolívar, making the revered Venezuelan figure come alive and step out of history's pages.

In 1994, García Márquez released a new collection of short stories, entitled *Strange Pilgrims*. All the stories feature Latin American protagonists, living in Europe—in Italy, Spain, France, and elsewhere. Just as García Márquez once found himself alone in Europe, so do his characters struggle in their new environment. That same year, García Márquez also completed *Love and Other Demons*, a novel about a love affair between a priest and a young woman who has fallen ill.

García Márquez's journalistic writing also experienced a boom in the 1990s and 2000s, in response to a series of national and international events. In 1999, García Márquez bought a news magazine, *Cambio*, which was based in Bogotá. The weekly periodical had been struggling financially since it was established five years earlier, but García Márquez's investment helped rejuvenate it. García Márquez not only became the chief owner, but also the magazine's editorial board director and main reporter. García Márquez was fulfilling a lifelong dream. When he won the Nobel Prize in 1982, he had planned to use the prize money to start his own news magazine, but he had trouble launching the project. He had thus saved the money and waited for the right opportunity, which finally came along with *Cambio*.

JOURNALISTIC ROOTS

Journalism was always central to García Márquez's life. He frequently referred to himself as a journalist who merely wrote fiction as a hobby. "I'm a journalist," he once said in an interview. "I've always been a journalist. My books couldn't have been written if I weren't a journalist because all the material was taken from reality."[101]

He often wrote about the rise in drug trafficking between Colombia and the United States, about which he holds strong opinions. "All the money that Colombia invests in fighting drugs should be invested in the United States to research synthetic cocaine,"[102] he once told a reporter, suggesting that the sheer demand for drugs from the United States was what fueled the drug trade in Colombia. He also continued to defend and support the Cuban government. In late 1999, a young boy was found floating in a life preserver off the coast of Florida. Badly sunburned, unconscious, and dying of thirst, Elian Gonzalez had been part of a group of Cubans fleeing the island, hoping to find a better life in the United States. Their flimsy boat had capsized in the rough waters, and the boy's mother, Elizabeth (who had brought Elian on the trip without telling the boy's father), had died. The boy's father, Juan Gonzalez, wanted his son to come home to Cuba immediately.

The story of Elian Gonzalez revealed the longstanding tensions between Cuba and the United States. Elian's relatives, who lived in Florida and had been U.S. citizens for many years, wanted the boy to stay with them, believing that it had been his mother's dying wish for her son to become an American. Juan Gonzalez was furious not only that his son had been kidnapped and put into grave danger, but that now he was not being permitted to return to Cuba. Gonzalez demanded that the U.S. government force Elian's relatives in Miami, Florida, to return Elian to Cuba.

Writing in the *New York Times*, García Márquez offered his opinion on the matter, saying, "Nobody in Miami seems to care about the harm being done to Elian's mental health by the cultural uprooting to which he is being subjected. . . . In other words, the real shipwreck of Elian did not take place on the high seas, but when he set foot on American soil."[103] Elian's Miami relatives were eventually forced by the U.S. government to give up Elian, who was returned to his father and his stepmother in Cuba.

Ironically, García Márquez's editorial in the *New York Times* appeared at the same time that a rumor was spreading that he was dying. In 1999, García Márquez was diagnosed with lymphatic cancer and began intensive medical treatment. On May 29, 2000, a poem entitled "La Marioneta" ("The Puppet") appeared in the Peruvian newspaper *La Republica*.

Signed by García Márquez, the poem seemed to be a farewell to his friends and family:

> *If for a moment God would forget that I am a rag doll and give me a scrap of life, possibly I would not say everything that I think, but I would definitely think everything that I say.*
> *I would value things not for how much they are worth but rather for what they mean. . . .*
> *If God would bestow on me a scrap of life, I would dress simply, I would throw myself flat under the sun, exposing not only my body but also my soul.*

News spread rapidly through South America that García Márquez was dying. The poem appeared in the newspapers of many other countries in the region, along with articles about his impending death. The Internet also helped spread the rumor. People throughout the world began mourning the last days of García Márquez as the poem was translated into other languages and circulated. Colleagues and friends discussed in interviews in newspapers, on the radio, and on television how they were heartbroken by the news.[104]

Eventually, the rumor was revealed to be a hoax. The poem turned out to be the work of a Mexican ventriloquist, written for his stage act. Somehow—and how this happened is unclear—García Márquez's name became attached to the poem when it was published and, combined with the factual information about his struggle with cancer, the rumor spread like wildfire. García Márquez never commented either on the poem or the hoax. He continued to write and to receive treatment for his illness. His article on Elian Gonzalez confirmed to the world that he was indeed still alive and well.

García Márquez continues to spend his time between his homes in Mexico City, Bogotá, Cartagena, Havana, and others in Europe. He maintains a strict writing schedule, routinely waking at 5:00 A.M. He writes steadily in his home office all morning and for most of the afternoon, and then spends the

Gabriel García Márquez's wife, Mercedes, remained a loyal supporter of her husband through the years of poverty and hardship. The couple, pictured here at the Havana Film Festival in 2003, have two children—Rodrigo and Gonzalo.

rest of the day giving interviews, visiting friends, attending meetings, or relaxing with his family.

In 2003, his long-awaited memoir, *Living to Tell the Tale*, was published. In it, he offered personal thoughts on his life and experiences, once again justifying his well-earned reputation as a man who is a hero in his own country and around the world, and a true living legend.

Chronology and Timeline

1899–1902 The War of a Thousand Days, Colombia's worst civil war, is fought between Liberals and Conservatives.

1927 Gabriel García Márquez is reportedly born on March 6 in Aracataca.

1928 Hundreds of banana workers are killed by the Colombian military during a general strike against the American United Fruit Company.

1940 Gabriel García Márquez wins scholarship to the Liceo Nacional de Zipaquirá, near Bogotá.

1947 Enrolls in the law school of the Universidad Nacional in Bogotá; his first short story, "The Third Resignation," is published in *El Espectador*.

1948 Witnesses the assassination of Jorge Eliécer Gaitán; the era of *La Violencia* begins in Colombia and lasts almost 10 years.

1927
Gabriel García Márquez born on March 6 in Aracataca

1947
His first short story, "The Third Resignation," is published in *El Espectador*

1956
Stranded in Paris and writes *In Evil Hour* and *No One Writes to the Colonel*

1927   1958

1940
Wins scholarship to the Liceo Nacional, near Bogotá

1948
Witnesses the assassination of Jorge Eliécer Gaitán

1958
Marries Mercedes Barcha

1950 Leaves law school and begins a full-time career in journalism; meets the other members of the Barranquilla Group.

1955 *Leaf Storm*, his first book, is published; writes the account of sailor Luis Alejandro Velasco's survival at sea and exposes the military's cover-up, which angers the Colombian government; the news offices of *El Espectador* are shut down by the authorities.

1956 Stranded in Paris and writes the manuscripts of what will eventually be published as *In Evil Hour* and *No One Writes to the Colonel*.

1958 Marries Mercedes Barcha.

1959 The Cuban Revolution erupts and García Márquez supports its cause.

1959
Cuban Revolution erupts and García Márquez supports its cause

1974
Founds *Alternativa* magazine

1985
Love in the Time of Cholera is published

1959   2003

1965
Goes into seclusion for more than a year to write *One Hundred Years of Solitude*

1982
Awarded the Nobel Prize for Literature

2003
Publishes the first volume of his memoirs, *Living to Tell the Tale*

1961 Accepts a job with *Prensa Latina* and moves to New York to be the American correspondent; resigns from *Prensa Latina* and makes a bus trip through the American South; moves his family to Mexico City.

1962 Wins a national fiction award for *In Evil Hour*; disassociates himself from *In Evil Hour*, which is published in edited form by a Spanish publisher; he experiences a three-year writing slump.

1965 Goes into seclusion for 18 months to write *One Hundred Years of Solitude*.

1967 *One Hundred Years of Solitude* is published and immediately becomes a best-seller.

1970 *One Hundred Years of Solitude* is published in English.

1974 Founds *Alternativa* magazine.

1975 Publishes *The Autumn of the Patriarch*; becomes a close friend of Cuban leader Fidel Castro.

1980 Convinces Fidel Castro to allow poet Heberto Padilla to leave Cuba.

1981 Publishes *Chronicle of a Death Foretold*.

1982 Awarded the Nobel Prize for Literature.

1985 *Love in the Time of Cholera* is published.

1990 Publishes *The General in His Labyrinth*, a historical novel about Simón Bolívar.

1994 Publishes *Strange Pilgrims* and *Love and Other Demons*.

1999 Buys *Cambio*, a news magazine; the case of Elian Gonzalez, a Cuban refugee, causes renewed United States–Cuban tensions; writes articles supporting the return of Elian Gonzalez to his family in Cuba; diagnosed with lymphatic cancer.

2000 Rumor of his death circulates, but is proven to be a hoax.

2003 Publishes the first volume of his memoirs, *Living to Tell the Tale*.

2005 Colombian authorities craft a plan to make Aracataca and the childhood home of García Márquez a tourist attraction.

Notes

Chapter 2

1 Gabriel García Márquez, *Living to Tell the Tale,*. trans. Edith Grossman, (New York: Vintage Books, 2004), 44.

2 Raymond Williams, *Gabriel García Márquez* (Boston: Twayne Publishers, 1984), 7.

3 Mario Vargas Llosa, "Garcia Marquez: From Aracataca to Macondo," *Gabriel García Márquez: Modern Critical Views*, ed. Harold Bloom (New York: Chelsea House Publishers, 1989), 6.

4 García Márquez, *Living to Tell the Tale*, 36.

5 Llosa, 6.

Chapter 3

6 Allen B. Ruch, "The Uncertain Old Man Whose Real Existence Was the Simplest of His Enigmas." Available online at *http://www.themodernword.com/gabo/gabo_biography.html*

7 García Márquez, *Living to Tell the Tale*, 55.

8 Ibid., 50.

9 Ibid., 54–55.

10 Ibid., 51.

11 Ibid., 57.

12 Ibid., 65.

13 Ibid., 66.

14 Ibid.

15 Ibid., 67.

16 Ibid.

17 Jon Lee Anderson, "The Power of Gabriel García Márquez," *The New Yorker*, September 27, 1999. Available online at *http://www.themodernworld.com/gabo/gabo_power.html*.

18 Llosa, 7.

19 García Márquez, *Living to Tell the Tale*, 83.

20 Peter H. Stone, "The Art of Fiction," *Paris Review*, Number 82, Winter 1981, 56.

21 García Márquez, *Living to Tell the Tale*, 85.

22 Llosa, 7.

Chapter 4

23 Leslie Jermyn, *Colombia* (Milwaukee: Gareth Stevens Publishing, 1999), 12.

24 García Márquez, *Living to Tell the Tale*, 86.

25 Ibid., 99–100.

26 Ibid., 107.

27 Ibid., 135.

28 Ibid., 136.

29 Ibid., 139.

30 Ibid., 142.

Chapter 5

31 Ibid., 156.

32 Ibid.

33 Ibid., 158.

34 Ibid., 198.

35 Ibid., 208.

36 Ibid., 213.

37 Ibid., 225.

38 Anderson, "The Power of Gabriel García Márquez."

39 Ibid.

40 García Márquez, *Living to Tell the Tale*, 261.

41 Ibid.

42 Ibid., 261–262.

Chapter 6

43 Ibid., 270.

44 Ibid., 272.

45 Ibid., 273.

46 Ibid., 274.

47 Ibid., 275.

48 Ibid.

49 Ibid., 276.

50 Jermyn, *Colombia*, 12.

51 Ibid.

52 García Márquez, *Living to Tell the Tale*, 305.

53 Ibid., 306.

Chapter 7

54 Ibid., 307–312.

55 Jermyn, *Colombia*, 12.

56 García Márquez, *Living to Tell the Tale*, 326.

57 Ibid., 326.

58 Ibid., 366.

59 Ibid., 385.

60 Ibid., 400.

61 Ibid., 518.

62 Ibid., 522.

63 Ibid., 524.

64 Ibid., 525.

Chapter 8

65 Silvana Paternostro, "One Hundred Reflections: An Oral Biography of Gabriel García Márquez." *The Week*. Available online at *http://www.the-week.com/23Nov16/life2.htm.*

66 García Márquez, *Living to Tell the Tale*, 419.

67 Paternostro, "One Hundred Reflections: An Oral Biography of Gabriel García Márquez."

68 García Márquez, *Living to Tell the Tale*, 488.

69 Ibid., 532.

70 Ibid., 533.

71 Llosa, "Garcia Marquez: From Aracataca to Macondo," 12.

72 Ibid., 284.

Chapter 9

73 Anderson, "The Power of Gabriel García Márquez."

74 Ibid.

75 Ibid.

76 Ibid.

77 Ruch, "The Uncertain Old Man."

78 Ibid.

79 Llosa, "Garcia Marquez: From Aracataca to Macondo," 15.

Chapter 10

80 Ruch, "The Uncertain Old Man"; Llosa, "Garcia Marquez: From Aracataca to Macondo," 16.

81 Ruch, "The Uncertain Old Man."

82 Ibid.

83 Ibid.

84 Ibid.

85 Harold Bloom, ed. *Modern Critical Views: Gabriel Garcia Marquez* (New York: Chelsea House Publishers, 1989), 285.

86 Llosa, "Garcia Marquez: From Aracataca to Macondo," 17.

87 Regina James, "Liberals, Conservatives, and Bananas: Colombian Politics in the Fictions of Gabriel Garcia Marquez." *Gabriel Garcia Marquez: Modern Critical Views* (New York: Chelsea House Publishers, 1989), 125.

Chapter 11

88 Paternostro, "One Hundred Reflections: An Oral Biography of Gabriel García Márquez."

89 Bloom, 285.

90 Ruch, "The Uncertain Old Man."

91 Anderson, "The Power of Gabriel García Márquez."

92 Ruch, *http://www.themodern-word.com/gabo/gabo_ works_ fiction.html#Anchor-The-23240).*

93 Bloom, 285.

94 Anderson, "The Power of Gabriel García Márquez."

95 David Streitfeld, "The Intricate Solitude of Gabriel García Márquez," *Washington Post*, April 10, 1994, F1. Available at ProQuest Direct Database.

96 Anderson, "The Power of Gabriel García Márquez."

97 The Nobel Prize Web site. Available online at *http://nobel-prize.org/literature/laure-ates/1982/*

98 Ibid.

99 Paternostro, "One Hundred Reflections: An Oral Biography of Gabriel García Márquez."

100 Ibid.

101 "Celebrated Colombia Writer Returns," Associated Press, January 25, 1999. Available online at *http://www.themodernworld.com/gabo/cambio.html.*

102 James Brooke, "Cocaine's Reality, by García Márquez," *New York Times*, March 11, 1995, A3.

103 Gabriel García Márquez, "Shipwrecked on Dry Land," *New York Times*, March 29, 2000, A25. Available online at ProQuest Direct Database.

104 Alex Boese, "Gabriel García Márquez's Final Farewell." Available online at *http://www.museumofhoaxes.com /marquez.html.*

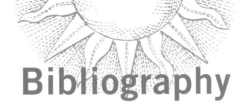

Bibliography

Books and Articles

Bloom, Harold, ed. *Gabriel García Márquez: Modern Critical Views.* New York: Chelsea House Publishers, 1989.

García Márquez, Gabriel. *Living to Tell the Tale.* Translated by Edith Grossman. New York: Vintage Books, 2004.

———. *One Hundred Years of Solitude.* New York: Harper Perennial, 2004.

Green, W. John. "'Vibrations of the Collective': The Popular Ideology of Gaitanismo on Colombia's Atlantic Coast, 1944–1948." *The Hispanic American Historical Review*, Volume 76, Issue 2 (May 1996): 283–311.

James, Regina. "Liberals, Conservatives, and Bananas: Colombian Politics in the Fictions of Gabriel Garcia Marquez." *Gabriel Garcia Marquez: Modern Critical Views.* Edited by Harold Bloom. New York: Chelsea House Publishers, 1989.

Jermyn, Leslie. *Colombia.* Milwaukee, Wisc.: Gareth Stevens Publishing, 1999.

Llosa, Mario Vargas. "Garcia Marquez: From Aracataca to Macondo." *Gabriel Garcia Marquez: Modern Critical Views.* Edited by Harold Bloom. New York: Chelsea House Publishers, 1989.

Stone, Peter H. "The Art of Fiction." *Paris Review*, Number 82, Winter 1981, 56.

"William Faulkner." *The Norton Anthology of American Literature.* New York: W. W. Norton and Company, 1998.

Williams, Raymond. *Gabriel García Márquez.* Boston: Twayne Publishers, 1984.

Web sites

Anderson, John Lee. "The Power of Gabriel García Márquez." *The New Yorker.* September 27, 1999. Available online at *http://www.themodernword.com/gabo/gabo_power.html.*

Anderson, Perry. "A Magical Realist and His Reality." *The Nation.* January 26, 2004. Available online at *http://www.ssl.thenation.com/docprint.mhtml?I=20040126&s= anderson.*

Bell-Villada, Gene. "Journey to Macondo in Search of García Márquez." *Boston Review.* Available online at *http://www.bostonre-view.net/BR08.2/villada.html.*

Boese, Alex. "Gabriel García Márquez's Final Farewell." Available online at *http://www.museumofhoaxes.com/marquez.html.*

Brooke, James. "Cocaine's Reality, by García Márquez." *New York Times,* March 11, 1995, p. A3. Available online at *http://www.pro-quest.com/.*

"Celebrated Colombia Writer Returns." Associated Press. January 25, 1999. Available online at *http://www.themodernworld.com/gabo/cambio.html.*

"Gabriel García Márquez." Books and Writers. Available online at *http://www.kirjasto.sci.fi/marquez.htm.*

García Márquez, Gabriel. "Shipwrecked on Dry Land." *New York Times.* March 29, 2000, p. A25. Available online at *http://www.proquest.com/.*

———. "The Solitude of Latin America." Nobel Lecture, December 8, 1982. NobelPrize.org. Available online at *http://www.nobelprize.org/literature/laureates/1982/marquez-lecture-e.html.*

"Journey Back to the Source: An Interview with Gabriel García Márquez." *The Virginia Quarterly Review Online.* Translated by Gene Bell-Villada. Available online at *http://www.vqronline.org/viewmedia.php/prmMID/9129*

Marx, Gary. "Locals Aim to Transform Nobel Writer's Town into Tourist Destination." *Chicago Tribune.* September 25, 2005. Available online at *http://www.duluthnewstribune.com.*

Parker, Lonnae O'Neal. "A Writer's Magic Muse: Isabel Allende Mines Her Memory for the Crystals of a Greater Truth." *The Washington Post.* November 24, 2001, p. C1. Available online at *http://www.proquest.com/.*

Paternostro, Silvana. "One Hundred Reflections: An Oral Biography of Gabriel García Márquez." *The Week*. Available online at *http://www.the-week.com/23Nov16/life2.htm*.

Ruch, Allen B. "The Uncertain Old Man Whose Real Existence Was the Simplest of His Enigmas." Available online at *http://www.themodernworld.com/gabo/gabo_biography.html*.

Streitfeld, David. "The Intricate Solitude of Gabriel García Márquez." *Washington Post*, April 10, 1994, p. F1. Available online at *http://www.proquest.com/*.

Further Reading

Books and Articles

Bell-Villada, Gene. *García Márquez: The Man and His Work*. Chapel Hill, N.C.: University of North Carolina Press, 1990.

Dolan, Sean. *Gabriel García Márquez*. New York: Chelsea House, 1994.

García Márquez, Gabriel. *In Evil Hour*. Translated by Gregory Rabassa. New York: Harper Collins, 1991.

———. *Leafstorm and Other Stories*. Translated by Gregory Rabassa. New York: Harper Collins, 1979.

———. *Love in the Time of Cholera*. Translated by Edith Grossman. New York: Alfred A. Knopf, 1988.

Web sites

Gabriel García Márquez Resources
http://www.levity.com/corduroy/marquez.htm

The Modern Word. "Gabriel García Márquez."
http://www.modernword.com

Gabriel García Márquez, Nobel Prize Web site
http://nobelprize.org/literature/laureates/1982/index.html

Commentary: Meeting Gabriel García Márquez
http://www.npr.org/templates/story/story.php?storyId=1495140

Index

Alternativa (magazine), 86
Anderson, Jon Lee, 38
Anderson, Sherwood, 72
Angulo, Guillermo, 74
Aracataca, Colombia, 19, 34
  birthplace, 9, 11, 14,
    20–21
  childhood in, 21–23,
    31–32, 57, 81–62
  economy, 12, 14–15, 81
  founders of, 16–17
  home museum in, 81
  model for fiction, 58, 67,
    75–76, 78, 81–82
  return to, 57
  superstitions of, 21
  tourism in, 81
Autumn of the Patriarch, The
  influence of power in, 85
  publication, 85
Awards and honors
  and the Nobel prize,
    89–92, 94
  for *One Hundred Years of
    Solitude*, 79–80

Barranquilla, Colombia, 11,
  62
  childhood in, 32, 34–36
  years in, 53–55, 57
Barranquilla Group
  members of, 53–55,
    57–58, 74
Batista, Fulgencio, 68, 70
Bay of Pigs, 71
Betancur, Belisario, 91
Big Mama's Funeral, 83
  publication, 74
Bogotá, 36, 50
  rioting in, 28, 51, 58
  years in, 40–47, 53, 58–59,
    71, 74, 86, 89, 96
Bolívar, Simón, 25, 27–28
  in fiction, 93–94
Borda, Eduardo Zalana, 42,
  45
Borges, Jorge Luis, 8

Calderón, Carlos Julio, 37–38
Cambio (magazine), 94
Cantato General (Neruda),
  44

Carranza, Eduardo, 45
Cartagena, Colombia, 11,
  58–59
  years in, 52, 57
Casa, La
  writing of, 56–57
Castro, Fidel
  friendship with Márquez,
    51, 70, 86, 88–89
  government, 86–87, 89
  revolution, 65, 68, 70–71,
    87
childhood
  birth, 9, 15, 20–21, 29, 81
  with grandparents, 21–25,
    27, 30–31, 57, 81–82
  with parents, 30–39
Chronicle of a Death Foretold
  publication, 89
  Santiago Nasar in, 89
Ciénaga, Colombia, 13
*Cien años de soledad. See One
    Hundred Years of
    Solitude*
Colegio San Jose, 35–36
Colombia, 39–40
  civil war, 10, 18, 25, 27–29
  diversity, 9–11, 36
  drug trade, 94–95
  economy, 25, 28
  government, 12–13,
    25–29, 38, 45–47, 51,
    58–61, 81–82, 89, 95
  history of in fiction, 8, 13
  independence, 25, 28
  journalism, 52
  literature, 42, 45, 53–54,
    74, 83, 88, 92
  military, 13–14, 53, 59, 89
  social inequity in, 12
  superstitions in, 11
  La Violencia in, 28–29,
    51–53, 58, 67–68
Communism, 44, 60, 65
  in Colombia, 68–69, 89
  in Cuba, 68, 70, 73, 86–87,
    89
Conservative Party
  government, 13, 18,
    25–26, 28–29, 38, 46,
    51
Cuban Revolution, 65
  events of, 68–75

education
  in Barranquilla, 32, 34–36
  law school, 8, 40–41,
    45–46, 48, 51–53, 57,
    68–69
  at Liceo Nacional de
    Zipaquíra, 36–40
Eli, Maroa Luisa, 91
Espectador, El (magazine)
  articles for, 58–61
  closing of, 61
  short stories in, 42, 45, 53
Espinosa, Jorge Álvara, 43
"Eva Is Inside Her Cat"
  (short story)
  publication, 45

Faulkner, William
  influence on Márquez, 8,
    54, 57, 67, 72–73
  The Sound and the Fury,
    72
Film industry
  work for, 73–74, 78–79
For Whom the Bell Tolls
  (Hemingway), 65, 67
Franco, Francisco, 44, 85
Freud, Sigmund, 37
Fuenmayor, Alfonso, 53–54,
  57
Fuentes, Carlos, 79

*Gabriel García Márquez: The
    Story of a Deicide*
  (Llosa), 83
Gaitán, Jorge Eliécer
  assassination of, 28, 48–52
  politics of, 46–47, 49–51
García, Gabriel Eligio
  (father)
  courtship, 16–20
  financial problems, 34–35,
    37, 39
  influence on son, 33, 38
  occupation, 17, 19, 21,
    31–32, 34
  politics, 18
  reputation, 17
*General in His Labyrinth,
    The*
  publication, 93
  Simón Bolívar in, 93–94

Gómez, Laureano, 29
Gonzalez, Elian, 95–96
Gonzalez, Juan, 95

Hemingway, Ernest, 8, 54
    For Whom the Bell Tolls,
        65, 67
    The Old Man and the Sea,
        65
    suicide, 65
    The Sun Also Rises, 65, 67
Heraldo, El (newspaper)
    articles for, 55, 57
Heraza, Héctor Rojas, 52
Hojarasca, La. See Leaf
    Storm

Iguarán, Luisa Santiaga
    Márquez (mother), 21,
        31, 57
    courtship, 16–20
    financial problems, 34–35,
        37, 39
illnesses
    lymphatic cancer, 95–96
    pneumonia, 56
In Evil Hour (La Mala hora),
    83
    editorial problems, 7,
        74–75
    government oppression
        and violence in, 67
    publication, 7, 74–75
    writing of, 67, 71, 74
influences
    Barranquilla Group,
        54–55
    Colombian history, 15, 25,
        27–29, 38, 81–82
    grandparents, 21–25, 27,
        30–31, 33, 38, 78, 82
    literary, 8, 23, 41–42,
        44–45, 54, 65, 67,
        72–73
    parents, 33
    teachers, 37–38
Innocent Eréndira and Other
    Stories
    publication, 85

James, Regina, 82
Jermyn, Leslie, 26

Jimenez, Rafael Dario, 81
journalism years, 8, 46, 63,
    86
    collections, 85, 93–94
    at El Espectador, 58–61
    freelance, 67
    at El Heraldo, 55, 57
    at Momento, 68
    at Prensa Latina, 71, 73
    roots, 94–97
    at El Universal, 52–53, 57
Joyce, James, 54

Kafka, Franz, 45
    The Metamphosis, 23,
        41–42
Kennedy, John F., 70–71

Leaf Storm (La Hojarasca),
    67, 83
    publication, 58, 74
Leftist Revolutionary Union,
    50
Liberal Party
    government, 13, 18,
        25–26, 28–29, 38, 46,
        50–52, 62
Liceo Nacional de Zipaquíra
    schooling at, 36–40, 52
Living to Tell the Tale, 10
    publication, 97
Llosa, Mario Vargas
    Gabriel García Márquez:
        The Story of a Deicide,
        83
    on Márquez, 66, 82
    on the United Fruit
        Company, 11–12, 14
Lorca, Federico García, 44
Love in the Time of Cholera
    Fermina Daza in, 91
    Florentino Ariza in, 91
    popularity of, 93
    publication, 91
Love and Other Demons
    publication, 94

Magical realism
    and Márquez, 22–24, 78,
        80–82
Mala hora, La. See In Evil
    Hour

"Marioneta, La" (hoax
    poem), 96
Márquez, Gonzalo (son), 6
    birth, 74
Márquez, Mercedes Barcha
    (wife), 89
    courtship of, 62–64, 67
    marriage, 68, 77
    support of, 6–7, 71,
        76–79, 91
    travels, 72–73
Márquez, Rodrigo (son), 6,
    72
    birth, 71–72
Márquez, Tranquilina
    (grandmother), 27, 32
    death, 57
    disapproval of son-in law,
        17–19
    influence on Márquez,
        21–24, 78, 82
    stories, 21, 24, 78
    superstitions, 11, 21,
        23–24, 78
marriage, 68, 77
Martín, Carlos, 38
Marxism, 38, 70
Masetti, Jorge Ricardo, 71
Meja, Nicolás Ricardo
    Márquez (grandfa-
        ther), 52
    death, 31, 57
    disapproval of son-in law,
        17–19
    influence on Márquez, 21,
        24–25, 27, 30–31, 33,
        38, 82
    politics, 18, 25, 93–94
    stories, 14, 24–25, 27, 33,
        82
    veteran, 25, 27, 31, 47, 64,
        66
Mendoza, Plinio Apuleyo,
    71, 73
Metamphosis, The (Kafka),
    23, 41–42
Mexico City, Mexico
    years in, 6, 73, 76, 86, 89,
        91, 96
Momento (newspaper)
    articles for, 68

110

Nacional, El (newspaper), 53
Neruda, Jan, 44
Neruda, Pablo, 45
  Cantato General, 44
Nobel Prize for literature, 44,
  65, 72
  for Márquez, 89–92, 94
No One Writes to the Colonel,
  83
  based on grandfather, 64,
  66
  publication, 74
  writing of, 64, 66–67

Old Man and the Sea, The
  (Hemingway), 65
One Hundred Years of
  Solitude (*Cien años de*
  soledad)
  awards for, 79–80
  Buendia family in, 11, 82
  censorship of, 13
  Colombia history in, 13
  friends and family in,
  54–55
  Macondo in, 81–82
  publication, 79, 83–84
  reality with fantasy in,
  22–23, 78, 80–62
  Remedios the Beauty in,
  22
  seclusion while writing,
  6–7, 76–79
  success of, 79–80
  translations of, 79
  Ursula in, 22
Operation Carlota, 86

Padilla, Heberto, 86–88
Pérez, Ospina, 46
Pinilla, Gustavo Rojas, 29, 85
Pinochet, Augusto, 85
politics
  and Communism, 68–70,
  73, 86–89

and controversy, 73, 88,
  90–91
early interest in, 9, 25
effect on work, 29
and Gaitán, 46–47
and Marxism, 38
Prensa Latina (news agency)
  work for, 71

reputation, 6, 83, 97
Riohacha, Colombia, 19
Rojas, Jorje, 45
Ruch, Allen B., 28, 85

Samudio, Álvaro Cepeda,
  53–54
Santa Marta Massacre, 13–14
Santander, Francisco de
  Paula, 25–26
Sierra, Juan Roa, 49–51
"Solitude of Latin America,
  The" (Nobel speech),
  92
Sound and the Fury, The
  (Faulkner), 72
Spanish Civil War, 44
Stalin, Joseph, 85
Strange Pilgrims
  publication, 94
Sun Also Rises, The
  (Hemingway) 65, 67

"Third Resignation, The"
  (short story)
  publication, 42
travels
  to Europe, 58, 74, 86–87,
  96
  to Havana, 88, 91, 96
  to Mexico, 6, 73, 76, 91, 96
  stranded in Europe,
  61–64, 67–69
  to United States, 71–73
Trujillo, Rafael, 85

United Fruit Company
  in Colombia, 10–12,
  14–15, 81
  Macondo, 57
  union strike, 12–13, 50, 82
Universal, El (newspaper), 57
  censorship of, 53
  Márquez's articles for,
  52–53
Universidad Nacional de
  Bogotá
  law school, 40–41, 45–46

Vargas, Carlos Cortés, 13
Vargas, Germán, 53–54, 57
Vega, Domingo Manuel,
  41–42
Velasco, Luis Alejandro
  articles on, 59–60
  shipwreck survivor, 58–60
Venezuela, 68, 71, 85, 94
Vinyes, Ramon, 54–55

War of a Thousand Days
  events of, 10, 18, 25,
  28–29
When I Was Happy and
  Uninformed
  publication, 85
Williams, Raymond
  biographer of Márquez,
  10–11
Woolf, Virginia, 54
World War I, 65
World War II, 39
writing slump, 7–8
writing style
  devotion to, 75, 97
  fantasy and reality, 22–24,
  78, 80–82, 90
  and literary influences, 45,
  67

Zabala, Clemente Manuel, 53

About the Author

Susan Muaddi Darraj is associate professor of English at Harford Community College in Bel Air, Maryland, where she teaches creative writing and literature. Her book *Scheherazade's Legacy: Arab and Arab American Women on Writing* was published by Praeger in 2004. She is also the managing editor of *The Baltimore Review*, a literary journal of poetry, fiction, and creative nonfiction.

Picture Credits